Through My Looking Glass

Volume II

Jan Bono

Sandridge Publications
www.JanBonoBooks.com

Best Wishes!
Jan Bono

First Printing, Fall 2012

Printed in the United States of America
Gorham Printing, Centralia, WA 98531

Cover Photo: North Head Lighthouse by Sheri Kent

Sandridge Publications
P.O. Box 278
Long Beach, WA 98631

http://www.JanBonoBooks.com

ISBN: 978-0-9838066-8-4

Dedication

To Anna Marie, my lifelong faithful sidekick,
and to all those readers with friends and family
they've often threatened to write about.
Enjoy!

Introduction

A good story is forever a good story, no matter when it's written or read. The stories contained herein are all gleaned from my former personal experience newspaper column, circa 1991-2002. My former readers will no doubt enjoy revisiting these tales in their original form, and I ask that new readers please forgive the occasional references to people, businesses, and days gone by.

Jan Bono
September, 2012

Contents

CHAPTER ONE
Special Occasions

Star-Spangled Soiree

"What can I get Jan for her birthday?" lamented Brittany. "What doesn't she already have?"

"Pasties," said Julie, without the slightest hesitation.

Brittany shrieked with demonic delight. "That's perfect! I can make them myself!"

And she did.

First, she cut out two six-inch circles of tag board. She used a neon yellow highlighter pen to color one side. Then she cut a line to the center of each one, overlapped the edges about an inch, and stapled them back together forming two shallow 'cups.'

The most difficult part came next. Using a glue stick, Brittany painstakingly pasted over 200 gold foil stars of various sizes to each cone. Gold tassels, the kind similar to those found on curtain valances, completed her design. She attached a tassel to the center of each shimmering orb with a length (*quite a length*) of gold cord.

With great fanfare, Brittany handed me her present during a celebratory get-together at my house a few days later. The likeness of 'Barbie' on the gift bag was a definite tip-off that Britt was up to something. That, and the fact that too many people gathered eagerly around as I dug through the tissue paper and extracted her creations.

The group laughed uproariously as I held them up.

"You don't already have some, do you?" Britt queried in a voice that suddenly sounded suspiciously southern-tinged. She batted her eyelashes at me in mock innocence. "It was Julie's suggestion. She said she was pretty sure you didn't already have a pair."

"Oh sure," mumbled Julie, elbowing Britt, "try to pin the blame on me…"

"What are they?" asked one fellow in the group. "They look like Chinese coolie graduation hats."

"They're pasties," I replied. "Birthday pasties.

"And no," I directed the second part of my remark to Brittany, "I didn't already have a pair. Thank you ever-so-much."

"Pastries?" continued the first fellow.

"Pasties," I corrected, enunciating as clearly as possible while laughing. "No 'R.'" I held them up against my chest to demonstrate. The tassels dangled a foot lower.

"Oh!" The man laughed, completely red-faced. "Oh… My!"

"Aren't you going to wear them?" asked Julie, as I set them next to a growing collection of greeting cards.

"Unfortunately," I said, sighing deeply and giving her a sad little shake of my head, "there's no way to attach them. I guess we'll all just have to admire them right there on the dining room table."

"Wanna bet?" asked Brittany. Gleefully, she dug deeper into the gift bag and produced a roll of double-sided scotch tape.

Ever the good sport, I fastened the cones to the front of my blouse and paraded, with a self-styled rendition of a bump and a grind, into the living room, leaving a trail of shiny shedded stars in my wake. The hoots and jeers, raucous laughter and wild applause was nearly deafening as I attempted to swing the tassels in opposite directions.

"There's someone at the door!" (*Exactly who said it, I'm still not sure, but if I ever find out…*)

With an exaggerated flourish, I swooped up a magnum of champagne on the way to answer the bell. I swung the door open wide, and came face-to-face with my pastor and his wife, who stood on the front porch doing an awfully realistic impression of guppies: Mouths open, mouths closed, mouths open, mouths closed, and no sound coming from either of them.

I recovered first: "Did I tell you that tonight we'd be having a Madonna look-alike contest?"

Thank goodness they both know me so well.

The major challenge of the next few hours was trying to keep the tassels out of the punch bowl while I played hostess.

And then it was time to serve the birthday cake. "This," I said, swinging my tassels to illustrate the point, "is just about as crazy as I get." I waited patiently until the room quieted.

"As you all may have noticed, these are not your ordinary pasties, nor am I your ordinary stripper." Laughingly, I waved the cake knife in Britt and Julie's direction. "By the way, girls, I know you live…

"Therefore," I continued, "I hope you all won't be too disappointed, but there will be no further floor show this evening."

An exaggerated sigh of relief blew out all 43 candles on the cake.

Turkey on the Mountain

It's going to be quiet at my house this Thanksgiving. Very quiet. Although, at the time of this writing, my relatives are all speaking in civilized tones, each of us has plans to "do our own thing" the fourth Thursday of November.

I've "done my own thing" on many Thanksgivings. I've casino-hopped in Reno, curled up at home with a good book and an even better pumpkin cheesecake, soaked in a hot tub in Lincoln City, and chained myself to my computer keyboard to write, write, write.

I've also "done other people's things" on Thanksgiving. I've spent the day car shopping, pheasant hunting in eastern Washington, and freezing my buns off in a football stadium.

But one notable Thanksgiving was the first Thanksgiving I was the M-word. (*Yes, I was married once, but I've been in recovery for that now for more years than I was married, so I don't think it should be held against me...)*

Anyway, I should have known trouble was brewing when my intended insisted we tie the knot on the only weekend between deer and elk seasons.

After a quick honeymoon trip down the Oregon coast, Mr. Ex informed me he would be spending our first wedded Thanksgiving on the back side of Saddle Mountain, elk hunting with his former in-laws and an assortment of old Tillamook buddies. It was a tradition, he said.

No problem, I thought. *I can show him I'm as good a sport as any bride during the first month of marriage.* In hindsight, I should have realized the honeymoon was over.

The plan was for Mr. Ex to leave early in the week to help set up the base camp. Since none of the trailer stoves could accommodate a whole turkey, I'd bring it with me Thursday morning—fully cooked—right out of the oven. The other provisions of our feast would be "potluck" from the assemblage of hunters.

At the appointed hour I was transported, along with the turkey, up the snow-packed twists and turns of the coast range to the makeshift hunting lodge. So far, so good.

The trailers and campers were backed into a rough circle. Tarps were strung from one vehicle top to another, forming a pseudo-canopy. All the doors opened toward the center. A burning barrel kept the common area toasty warm. Rounds of tree trunks served as both tables and chairs and were split into firewood as needed.

Mid-day we spread our banquet among the fir boughs. And what a banquet! Most memorable of the eclectic taste offerings was a roaster pan brimming with *hamburger* gravy. "It's the only kind of gravy I know how to make," said the cook with a shrug.

After our feast, we headed out for the late afternoon hunt. Two hours of bouncing and bumping over rutted goat trails passing themselves off as roads took its toll on my bladder. "I've *got* to *go*," I whispered to Mr. Ex.

He gave me one of those looks—the kind that makes you want to apologize even if you know you haven't done a darn thing wrong. A steep snow bank hugged my side of the truck, a deep gulch graced his side. He stopped the pickup right where it was. "There's tissue in the glove compartment."

I edged my way around the vehicle. Finding no

shrub to protect my modesty, I squatted down behind the truck. Meanwhile, Mr. Ex checked in with the other hunters via the CB radio.

"Hurry up," he hollered. "One of the guys is about a quarter mile back around the bend and heading this way."

Now, I don't know for sure if guys can do this, but somehow I managed to stop what I was doing mid-stream. Frantically, I tried to hoist my undies, panty hose, long-johns and jeans back to their proper place. "Tell him to wait a minute!" I shrieked.

At that precise moment, the Demon of Divorce instigated initial contact. Mr. Ex slid the pickup into gear and took his foot off the brake, slowly rolling on down the road, away from the bride whose language now indicated a total lack of good sportsmanship.

The majority of my clothing still around my knees, I began to run after him like a duck to a corn feed. Above the maniacal laughter of Mr. Ex I could hear the engine of the approaching vehicle. I looked back over my shoulder only to discover that 40 or 50 feet of baby blue toilet paper trailed behind me.

That was also a quiet Thanksgiving weekend. Very, very quiet.

Christmas Bells, those Christmas Bells!

I cringed while playing back the message: "I was wondering if you would like to help us out by being a bell-ringer," said the voice on my answering machine. Immediately I started compiling an extensive list of excuses beginning with "I just don't have the time."

But the voice, I'll call him Dale, belonged to the Presbyterian choir director. Never underestimate the power of a Presbyterian choir director. He was gently insistent; it was obvious he was used to dealing with reluctant volunteers. "We'll practice when it's convenient to your schedule," he said. "I think we can get by with only three or four practices."

"Uh, Dale? Unless you count the first 12 measures of 'Born Free' on the piano, my formal education did not include learning to play a musical instrument."

"You'll be responsible for two bells—two notes," he said. "One for each hand."

My resolve waivered just long enough to give him the edge.

"It'll be a lot of fun," he continued. "You'll enjoy it."

"I'll make you a deal," I compromised, "I'll come to the first practice and when you see how hopeless I am, I won't take offense if you ask me not to come back."

At the first practice, Dale handed me the white cotton gloves and pointed out the 'A' and 'G' bells. "You won't have to make any bell changes for flats or sharps during either number."

Flats? Sharps? *Either* number? "You mean we're doing more than one song?"

Dale smiled patiently. "I wrote special arrangements for both 'Joy to the World' and 'Joseph, Dearest Joseph, Mine.'"

"I've never heard of the second one," I said honestly, "but the first one starts out 'Jeremiah was a bullfrog'... right?"

He knew I was teasing him.

I took my place among the other ding-a-lings and mumbled, "My only qualification for this job is my ability to count to four."

"You only need to count to three in the second one," said one woman.

Small consolation, I thought, for a person who had never quite mastered the art of reading music.

Dale discovered that fact a short time later. Even that did not deter him. He simply took my music and coded in the notes I was to play with felt-tipped highlighter pens.

Unfortunately, he coded the left hand pink and the right hand green. Big mistake. Living the last 18 years on the coast has subliminally influenced my brain. As any good sailor knows, it's 'red, right, returning' on the channel markers. Whenever I saw a pink note I automatically lifted my right hand instead of my left.

Undaunted, Dale re-coded all my notes blue. "Lines with the left hand, spaces with the right."

The next few minutes went by fairly well, until the woman on my right missed a beat and failed to ring her bell. The woman on my left elbowed me.

"That wasn't one of mine," I whispered.

"Pass it on," she whispered back, elbowing me again.

At the second practice Dale tried to get fancy with us. "Accent the melody line by striking those bells a bit harder, and ring the harmonizing notes softly."

"Right." I nodded in agreement. "...What's a melody line?"

By the third rehearsal I think Dale knew he'd be lucky if we all finished the music at the same time. He gave us one final instruction: "Remember, if you can keep from making faces and grimacing when you make a mistake, fewer people will know you've goofed up."

The day of the performance a whole flock of fluttering butterflies took up restless residence in my stomach. Or maybe it was a gaggle of moths. Whatever. I was thankful for the skirt around the table where our music rested; it hid my trembling knees.

The church was full of familiar faces. Not only was I about to make a total fool of myself, but I was going to do it in front of a house packed with people I knew.

"God help us," I muttered as I retrieved my bells from their protective case.

"He will," said one of the other women.

And He did.

I won't go so far as to say we were perfect—far from it. But after the performance I discovered a very comforting fact: Either no one in the audience was aware of our minor boo-boos and technical blunders, or no one chose to point them out to us for fear they'd be recruited next year.

Next year? Well, it really was kind of fun...

Dear Santa

Dear Santa,

How are you? I am fine. How is Mrs. Claus? And the elves? Please give the reindeer an extra carrot for me—we're all counting on them Christmas Eve!

I have been a very good girl this year. Very, very, very good. So good I've been almost boring, but that's a whole 'nother story…

Most everything I want I already have. My mother says I am entirely too spoiled and that I shouldn't bother you by writing this year. But this year I'm not writing just for me. This year I'm asking for you to bring something for a few little friends of mine.

You see, Santa, I'm worried about some of my fourth graders. So many of them don't believe in you. So many of them have stopped believing in magic altogether. It must be very sad for them, and even sadder for you. I can't begin to imagine what the world would be like if no one believed in hope, or love, or miracles.

Sometimes a child will quietly approach me and ask if I *personally* believe in Santa Claus. Being a teacher, a sacred trust is put on the line. Rest assured, Santa, I'll never let you down—I *always* tell them the absolute truth.

I tell them about the time I discovered the sleigh tracks in the backyard and counted 36 hoof prints in the snow. *("Thirty-six!" they exclaim, but four hooves times eight reindeer is 32!" "Don't forget Rudolph," I say, not missing the opportunity for an object lesson in multiplication.*)

I tell them about the time two of your elves knocked on our front door on December 23 and asked how late my family would be enjoying a fire in the fireplace the next evening. "We're members of Santa's Safety Committee," they explained. "Santa's suit is made of fire-retardant material, but he doesn't want to take any chances. Besides, we don't mind taking the time off to do this survey—it's a nice break from building toys all day!"

I tell them about the time I pulled on your beard when I was having my picture taken with you, and how I found nothing but ashes in my stocking Christmas morning, and how Mom made me clean the whole mess up before I could open *any* other presents. (By the way, thanks for not holding a grudge—I really enjoyed the new skis!)

And finally, Santa, I tell my children about all the years I've waited up, watched the sky, and tried to pick out the twinkling lights that meant your sleigh was nearing my house. I still do that, you know, but instead of falling asleep at the window and waking up with a crick in my neck, I crawl into bed and listen to Christmas music when I start getting too sleepy.

So what do I want for my little friends? It's the biggest gift I've ever asked for, but I don't know where else to turn. And even though it's asking a lot, I'm sure you'll find plenty of room for it in your sleigh.

Santa, dearest Santa, a great many of my children are in desperate need of an extra-large helping of Christmas Magic. They need hugs and smiles and pats on the back just for being who they are.

My kids need moms and dads and grandparents who will spend time with them sharing the joys of the holidays. They need family traditions like baking cookies and sending cards and caroling at the nursing homes. They need secret shopping trips and someone to take them to Sunday School to learn the *real* reason behind the season.

I realize this is a rather large request. Gigantic. Mammoth. Enormous. Colossal. But Christmas Spirit is not something we can legislate or order at the drive-through window. It takes a commitment of *time* and it's kind of tough to wrap. But it's worth it, Santa, you know it is. Our children are only children for a short time; they deserve our best.

Thank you, Santa, I know in my heart you'll do what you can.

Oh, and Santa, just one more thing: If there's space in your sack to tuck in a little something for me, could you please bring me a ticket to Hawaii? Like I said, I've been a very, very, *very* good girl…

Love and Kisses,

Jannie B.

The Governor's Christmas Card

A little over a year ago, with a heart full of seasonal joy and jubilation, I mailed out my personalized Christmas cards. For over two decades I have taken pride in designing uniquely homemade (*some may say "bizarre", or at the very least, "unusual"*) greetings, and last year was no different.

On the front of the card was an authentic, non-retouched photo of me, arm-in-arm with Governor Lowry. We're both smiling broadly. Inside the card, in my very own green felt-tipped script, the greeting read: "The Governor and I wish you the very merriest Christmas ever."

Never mind how, or when, I came by the picture. Just trust me when I say that there was absolutely NO trick photography involved. The Christmas card was the brainchild of a dyed-in-the-wool democrat; I simply could not pass up such a golden opportunity in a victorious election year. I took particular pleasure in mailing a few of these cards out to my Republican friends. (*Yes, for the first time, I'm publicly admitting to having a couple of those. . .)*

The responses were varied. Many hooted with delight:

"You never cease to crack me up, Jan."

"Atta girl!"

"I wish *I'd* thought of doing that!"

Other responses, you can guess from which political party, were not so enthusiastic:

"One of these days, JB, you're gonna get your butt

arrested for fraud."

I hastily checked into this. Apparently an elected official is public domain, and since I wasn't using his image to promote a cause or sell a product, I'm in the clear. Besides, I genuinely believe Governor Lowry would be more than happy to wish my friends a Merry Christmas; for the most part, they are really very nice people, voting records notwithstanding.

"Who was that elderly gentleman in the picture with you?" wrote one rather snide friend. "Is he British? Is that why you call him Governor?"

"Let's wait and see what you have to say about good old Mike *next year*," said another.

Well, it's hard to believe, but it's next year already, and I'm still a staunch supporter of the Gov. I can readily identify with the trials and tribulations he has faced since being elected. All too vividly I remember way back when I was the "M" word (*married*) and stared my first budget shortfall square in the face one January. Like Governor Lowry, it was an unexpected debt that I inherited. Like Governor Lowry, I vowed never to be blindsided like that again. I wasn't, and I trust he won't be.

But back to the subject at hand. . .

A few weeks ago I got out my Christmas card list and discovered one of last year's greetings stashed among the stickers and seals. On a fluke, I mailed it to the Governor, explaining my holiday prank. I'd heard he had a great sense of humor, and I thought he might get a kick out of it.

But as soon as the card left my possession at the post office, I began to worry. What if he *didn't* think it was funny?

The days passed into weeks, and I think I may have been expecting too much to assume that my innocuous little greeting card would actually make it into the same hands that run our state. So here on the 21st of December, I don't know if I should breathe a sigh of relief that no offense was taken, or be miffed because I got no response. I suppose it *was* asking a bit much for him to answer me personally. After all, he is a very busy man.

Perhaps I'll be more successful with this column. My columns have been known to show up in some of the strangest places. Maybe this one will somehow find its way through all the bureaucrat channels. If so, I'll not let this chance slip by:

Merry Christmas, Governor Lowry, and God Bless Us, Every One.

Happy 30th Birthday, Scott!

"As soon as I opened my mailbox I knew I'd been had," said Scott. "I thought, 'Jan's setting me up to get a column out of this.'"

He was right.

For months I'd been trying to figure how to get even with him for all the pranks he pulled on me during the past year. It had to be perfect; it had to be unexpected. "Revenge is a dish best served cold," I reminded myself.

I solicited advice from all quarters. I considered and rejected decorating his truck with "Just Married" signs and tin cans, tinseling his apartment, sending him a strip-tease telegram during an important business meeting, and signing him up for an Amway seminar. One of my darling sixth graders suggested that I invite him into the classroom, "and then we can egg him!"

As tempting as that last suggestion was, I abandoned it too. Finally, in early January, just weeks before his birthday, I hit upon a usable idea—but I needed help. I wrote a flyer outlining my plan and distributed it to my relatives and friends, who in turn passed it on to their relatives and friends. Somehow, an ad got placed in the personals column of The Daily Astorian; I was going to get help from people I didn't even know.

Scott's birthday landed on a Monday holiday this year, and another friend and I took him out for an innocent little dinner. He was suspicious. He didn't want to wear the pink carnation we got him. He insisted on taking his own vehicle to the restaurant. He kept looking over his shoulder.

"I hope you aren't too disappointed if it's just the three of us out for a nice meal and a birthday toast," I told him. After dinner we went to another establishment where I had earlier dropped off a big bouquet of birthday balloons. He relaxed, figuring that was all we were planning.

It wasn't until Tuesday that the other shoe fell. When he went to his post office box he found it crammed with dozens of birthday cards from women he doesn't remember meeting. Most of the greetings mentioned something personal about him, and congratulated him on "hitting the big 3-0."

Scott's female correspondents represented over 20 different zip codes. He received close to 70 cards. But he didn't let on that he'd gotten *any*. For two days he made me squirm. For two whole days I didn't know if the joke had sparked or fizzled. Had I written the right box number on the flyers? Hadn't he been to the post office yet? *Where were all those cards we mailed?*

I was distraught; was it all for nothing? My own mother had driven to 5 different towns late Thursday evening to mail cards she and her friends had written during the previous week. But for two days he didn't flinch, didn't mention his birthday, didn't let on that anything at all unusual had happened.

"Leave it to Scott," laughed one friend, "to make you the straight man for your own joke."

By Wednesday afternoon I was determined I would DIE before giving him the satisfaction of asking how many birthday cards he received. But later that night he admitted that the prank had been successful. We spent the better part of the evening laughing about some of the things written inside the cards. I have some *very* creative friends…

"We're even now," I said, giving him my best shot at a beguiling smile. "Even for last year's Karaoke fiasco, the rubber rat joke, and the tinsel trick."

"NO." Scott shook his head and tapped lightly on the pile of greeting cards on the table before him. "*It isn't over…*"

Now ordinarily that last sentence would have been the end of my column, and Scott would have gotten the final word. But this isn't ordinarily. I am a very competitive practical joker, and I'm *determined* to win this round.

On January 17th, Scott turned 27.

CHAPTER TWO
At Home and Abroad

Famous Potatoes

Blackfoot, Idaho's claim to fame is the just-off-the-beaten-path Potato Expo.

I am not kidding.

Right out front stands a muddy-brown 10-feet high and six-feet wide cement potato sculpture advertising that very fact.

The museum and kitchen combo, once an old train depot, looks a lot like an old train depot converted into a museum and kitchen combo. After touring the spud-centered gift shop (*theme magnets, coffee mugs, hot pads, trivets, key rings, etc.*), and viewing a video purporting to help you distinguish an *authentic* Idaho potato from an ordinary tuber, guests are invited to lunch at a 20-seat potato bar.

"Out-of-staters get free tators" says the sign next to the menu. And then the visitor far from home must make a most difficult decision: What to glop on top of that tator. Butter? Sour cream? Cheese? Chili? Chili *and* cheese? Broccoli? Broccoli *and* cheese? I noted with some relief that 'all of the above' was not an option.

Washed down with a soda or lemonade, the potato,

with whatever glopped on top, is quite filling. But for those still hungry, there are potato chip cookies, potato ice cream and potato fudge.

I passed on dessert. After all, I was just traveling through Blackfoot, Idaho. I didn't have emotional preparation time to work up the culinary courage for a direct assault on my taste buds.

It took me a half dozen years of Garlic Festival visitations to try garlic ice cream (*which I dearly love*), and garlic and chocolate chip cookies (*which I can take or leave*). But by and large, we don't grow garlic here.

Cranberries are another story. At the annual Cranberrian Fair I needed no encouragement to sample dried cranberries, cranberry catsup and cranberry fudge.

So now, being the Peninsula promoter that I am, I'm imagining a giant, 10-feet high and 10-feet wide, ruddy-red cement cranberry at the junction of highways 101 and 103. None of this one-shot weekend festival stuff, but a year-round 'expo' of the first order, complete with a full-time professionally trained staff. Local unemployment figures would plummet as scores of workers decked out in crane-berry hats gave our tourists the berries.

Picture this: Reader boards along the interstate, full-page ads in Sunset magazine, TV commercials during 'Seinfeld.' Our number one agricultural crop could put us up there with Yellowstone National Park and Mount Rushmore as vacation hot-spots.

And if not the cranberry, how about a 52-week Clamfest? Tour busses cruising the beach. Contestants vying for the honor of sculpting the world's largest clam doughnut. The daily prize for such a feat—a steaming bowl of chowder to take away the ocean chill.

We already have an enormous wooden clam posed coquettishly next to a gigantic frying pan. We already have several old train depots begging to be converted into a museum and kitchen combo. By twisting the Potato Expo's words around we already have the obvious slogan: "Free 'razors' for outta-staters" (*Oregon residents not included*).

Fish are another valuable local commodity. Visualize mammoth metallic silver salmon forming an arch across the roadway welcoming visitors to the magic kingdom of 'Salmon-ella.' Oops, I guess that idea could use a little refinement.

The major flaw I'm seeing in these plans is that—unlike the Idaho potato—cranberries, clams and silver salmon are not always in abundant supply. Perhaps we should focus on a resource more readily accessible.

I have it on good authority that most people who visit our area, regardless of the season, are quietly smuggling a little beach sand home with them in their shoes, cars and miscellaneous clothing. Later, steeped in remorse, these vacationers view their ocean side experience as one gargantuan guilt trip.

Couldn't we find a 'legal' way to celebrate the sand? Yes, I know we have 'Sandsations' in July, but I'm still thinking expo potential, which knows no seasonal slump. We've got the location, location, location, so how about working on the marketing, marketing, marketing? You just gotta have a gimmick.

In my mind's eye I can see and hear it now: Clever graphics in the Wall Street Journal, lights flashing on the Goodyear blimp, catchy jingles on every radio station in America. "Visit the Peninsula's 28-mile drivable snack bar: SAND-WHICH-IS there for everyone! Help yourself!"

The Potato Expo palls by comparison.

Neon Reverie

I dreamed I was in Las Vegas. A mysterious man named Michael met me at the airport in a white limousine. He spoke with an accent. As I settled into the rear of the limo, I settled in for a good long fantasy…

Through tinted windows I got my first glimpse of the infamous Vegas strip. A giant sphinx guarded the gates of the pyramid-shaped Luxor hotel. Just north of the pyramid was the medieval castle of Excalibur. Calypso music played outside the Tropicana. "Come see the exotic birds," said the sign advertising their wildlife walk. Across the way a mammoth MGM lion surveyed his kingdom.

Where in the world am I? My mind clouded with confusion. *Egypt? England? The tropical rain forest? A Hollywood movie studio?*

I hushed my inner critic. *I'm dreaming*, I reminded myself, *sit back and relax.*

Yet Caesar's Palace took my slumbering breath away. Intricate architecture consistent with the theme loomed larger-than-life both inside and out. When the colossal statues of the Roman gods came to animated life at the mall fountain, I was dumb-struck by the colorful laser lightning bolts that flashed across the darkened indoor sky.

In the Stage Deli at the Palace I met a dashing young writer named Tim, who was cleverly disguised as an amicable waiter. The menu's celebrated triple-decker sandwiches were named for the likes of David Letterman,

Buddy Hackett and George Foreman. One look at the picture on the wall and I knew even my big mouth couldn't handle a sandwich that size.

Tim served me kosher pickles, potato pancakes with applesauce and sour cream, and an authentic New York cheesecake.

"The lipstick is a sure sign that things are over," said Tim with a sigh, placing the bill on the table.

"Things?" I asked him coyly. "Could you be more specific? What kinds of things? A kiss? An evening tryst? An entire relationship?"

"Did I say things?" Tim smiled. For a character in a dream, he sure made great eye contact. "I simply meant that dinner was over," he admitted, "but now that you mention it, it is a pretty good line…"

We exchanged writing encouragement and best wishes on completing the next great American novel, and I wandered back out into the warm night.

At Treasure Island, safely hidden among the palm trees with a few hundred other people, I watched a pirate ship sink a British frigate. A few minutes later I narrowly escaped the volcanic eruption in front of the Mirage.

And speaking of mirages, about then the Statue of Liberty appeared smack-dab in the middle of my Vegas fantasy.

Only water stood between me and the majestic statue, and beyond her I gazed, open-mouthed, upon the fabulous New York skyline. A 14 million dollar roller coaster clogged up the view between the harbor lady and the Empire State Building, reminding me that nothing has to make sense when you're dreaming.

Inside the New York, New York casino, gaming tables dotted the landscape of Central Park, tucked between deciduous trees and penny-lined pristine ponds. Beyond the trees I could see the landmark “New York Slot Exchange.” The change carts bore an uncanny resemblance to yellow New York taxi cabs.

Greenwich Village beckoned with the smells of fresh pastries and dark coffee giving way to an aromatic assault of world cuisine served up at sidewalk cafés. A man in a dark turtleneck sweater played the blues in a small piano bar and I suddenly felt the urge to recite beat poetry on the street corner.

Regretfully, I left New York to continue my adventure. Temporarily overcoming my lifelong fear of heights, I rode an elevator to the top of the Stratosphere tower, 135 stories above the strip, in 37 seconds, flat. The windows of the enclosed observation deck started at my feet and tilted outward at a 45 degree angle. My acrophobia returned in a rush.

The Fremont Street Experience was well worth the trip downtown. An hourly light show transformed the canopy above several city blocks into a rippling screen of color and sound. Street musicians entertained between shows, one group turning garbage can lids, dust pans and five gallon plastic buckets into a viable toe-tapping band.

And everywhere, the music and bells and beeps and buzzes and glitz and glitter and shimmer and sparkle and whirling bars and spinning sevens and dancing diamonds and clustered cherries and flashing neon lights pushed me way, way, WAY beyond sensory overload.

It was time to wake up.

And so I did.

—IN LAS VEGAS!

Cruising on the Willapa

"Come on, Jan," implored George. "The boat leaves in 30 minutes."

"Thirty minutes!" I fairly shouted into the phone. "I can't possibly make it to Nahcotta in 30 minutes!"

"Okay," countered George, "make it in 45."

"No way," I said. "Maybe if you'd called earlier..."

"What else do you have to do today?" he queried.

"To start with, I've been putting off proofreading Rushford's new mystery novel; I've got 29 12-page term papers to correct; my brother is waiting for a reply as to whether I'll co-author a book with him; my publisher is anxious to see the first three chapters of my latest endeavor; the Sonics are playing—"

"All right already," interrupted George, "so can you be there in an hour?"

"*George*!"

"I thought you prided yourself on being spontaneous," he continued. "Set your VCR and catch the game later—there's nothing on that list of yours that can't be put off a few hours. When's the last time you had an opportunity to take a sunset cruise out on the Willapa?"

"I've never actually been boating on the bay," I admitted.

"That settles it," said George. "You're coming with us."

I sighed exaggeratedly. "What part of 'NO' don't

you understand?"

"Now you've only got 55 minutes," said George.

I arrived at the Port of Nahcotta exactly 52 minutes later.

"Smart money was on you not showing up," said George's friend Tom.

I gave Tom my best smile. "Then I guess SMART MONEY wouldn't have been so smart this time."

"You put up some good arguments, I'll give you that," said George as he helped me aboard. "But you'll be glad you're here. Work can wait; you needed a break."

Andy Wiegardt, skipper of the 43-foot custom-built Willapa Bay Excursions tour boat, settled his passengers and commenced introductions. Then he outlined several options on the type of sightseeing available that evening.

As we cleared the harbor and headed south, I clambered to the top deck along with most of the other cruisers. Andy passed around several pairs of binoculars while Tom, also an experienced sailor, took a turn at the wheel. The chart propped in front of Tom indicated the various depths of 'Shoalwater Bay.'

"The boat only draws 26 to 28 inches," said Andy, "so even when the tide's out navigation isn't all that difficult."

Easy for him to say, I thought, certain that if he offered *me* the chance to drive the boat, I'd be able to find the only significant sand bar in miles and manage to get us stuck in nothing flat.

Through the binoculars I recognized a few familiar homes along the west bank. An assortment of birds skimmed along the water in front of us. The sun caught what little wake the boat kicked up and made it glisten like a sparkling silver carpet. Then Andy pulled back the throttle, and the engine fell silent.

George put a blues tape into the stereo and the group climbed back down the ladder to share our assorted foodstuffs. Whether it was the salt air or the sense of adventure, our makeshift meal on the back deck of that boat tasted much better than many dinners I've had in four-star restaurants.

Our eclectic picnic included roast beef sandwiches, several kinds of cheese and crackers, salmon and cream cheese spread, bagels, papayas, grapes, baby carrots and homemade cinnamon rolls.

Andy, ever watchful, let us drift quietly while the sun set on our humble repast. I looked out at the lush green hills on Long Island and released a long, restful, contented sigh. All my tension, worries and miscellaneous mind-clutter was blown gently away by the early evening breeze.

"Glad you came?" asked George.

I simply smiled, took a few of the grapes from the cluster he offered and passed the rest on to Tom.

All too soon, Andy restarted the engines and we headed back to port. "I've been thinking about offering some special cruises this summer," he said. "Maybe a singles cruise, or a full moon cruise. How does that sound?"

"Theme cruises?" I asked, watching the last bit of color drain from the western sky. "That's a great idea! After all, today's cruise was designed to celebrate my birthday, wasn't it?"

"*Your birthday?!*" exclaimed Tom and George together.

"In truth, it's still a few days away," I replied, "but thanks to you guys, my 'Summer of 42' is off to a great start."

The Custer Connection

Shortly after noon on the 120th anniversary of what is now known by the politically correct 'Battle of the Little Bighorn,' I sat on a grassy hillside adjacent to the modern visitors' center and gift shop sampling barbecued buffalo meat and sipping a diet soda.

To my right was the national cemetery, the 50 star flag flying at half-mast. To my left was the knoll where George Armstrong Custer and a significant portion of the 7th Calvary met their destiny.

Below me, under a large blue awning, members of the Cheyenne and Sioux tribes spoke of their ancestors' reason for leaving the reservations to assemble along the Little Bighorn River 120 years ago: 'Peace through Unity.'

Television cameras rolled as a competition to select and construct a fitting memorial for the Indians was announced.

But this wasn't why I came.

I brushed off my slacks and walked quietly to my car. Driving along the five-mile meandering ridge-top road to observe the entrenchment of Major Marcus Reno and Captain Frederick Benteen, I searched for a sense of understanding.

In the Reno/Benteen parking lot I eavesdropped as two men stood in the hot sun, heads together, poring over an aerial map. They discussed with some animation their individual thoughts on the most famous battle in American history.

"Hello," I said, interrupting them, "where are you from, and how do you know so much about this place?"

"I'm from Chicago," said the taller of the two, "and like most everyone else, I've got a carload of books with me. I started out at Fort Lincoln, North Dakota and followed Custer's route here."

"I'm Bruce," said the second man, "from Denver. I just met Mitch an hour ago. We're going to work our way back to the main monument, stopping at each pull-out along the road. ...Want to join us?"

I readily accepted the offer, but I felt like a fraud—I only had one book with me, Dee Brown's "Showdown at Little Bighorn." I didn't admit I hadn't read "Son of the Morning Star," which was easily the most-quoted reference.

Nevertheless, our three-vehicle caravan, sporting license plates from Illinois, Colorado and Washington, took six hours to retrace the five miles back to the visitors' center. At each stop we spread out maps, took photos, and discussed in depth the progress and events of the 7th Calvary troops.

Where were the companies of Custer? Reno? Calhoun? Keogh? Terry? Up which gorge did Benteen retreat? From what vantage point did Weir abandon his plan to ride to Custer's defense?

Initially I felt 'historically challenged,' but not being particularly shy, I soon jumped in with my own barrage of questions. "Where was the body of newspaper correspondent Mark Kellogg found? Did Trooper Thomas O'Neill eventually become a surgeon? Was it true that Keogh's horse, Comanche, was carried by litter to the rescue boat?"

By the time we arrived at the mass grave of 220 cavalrymen, we three had formed an uncommon bond. With quiet reverence we observed the markers of 41 fallen soldiers surrounding what is assumed to be the last breath of George Armstrong Custer.

A thick haze rolled in from the river valley. A shiver moved involuntarily through the small remaining group gathered by the fence.

"One hundred twenty years ago," whispered Bruce, "right here...right now."

I glanced at Mitch—his eyes, like mine, were wet. He returned his video camera to its case, but continued to gaze at the names on the white tombstones dotting the hillside. "Sleep well," he murmured huskily.

The lump in my throat prevented me from saying anything at all. *This*, I thought, *this is why I came.*

We lingered till closing, unwilling to break the spell. Finally, park rangers ushered our vehicles out; the iron gates clanged shut behind us as the sun set.

At the crossroads, Bruce turned his truck north, toward Billings. I opted to drive south a few hours before calling it a day. Mitch had reservations at a nearby motel.

I left the battlefield with a strong sense of my heritage, my experience enhanced a thousand fold by a chance meeting with a Chicago accountant and a Denver electrician.

To these fine gentlemen I owe a large debt of gratitude for including this teacher/writer from the Washington coast in their personal pilgrimages. I appreciate them for so willingly sharing their time, expertise, compassion, and humor, but especially for their patience.

Thanks, guys.

The Strait Scoop

By some dubious twist of fortune, we arrived in Port Angeles just in time to board the evening ferry to Victoria, British Columbia. I'm still not sure what possessed me to agree to cross the Strait of Juan de Fuca after I learned that the gentle afternoon breezes had picked up to a brisk 60 knots.

"Piece of cake," said my traveling companion. "Nobody gets seasick on a ship this size."

I wasn't convinced.

"We're not going out into the ocean. It's really just an arm of Puget Sound. You'll be fine."

Oh, how I wanted to believe him.

We parked the car on the lower level and scrambled up several flights of stairs to a glass-enclosed observation deck. The seats were aligned in alternating rows facing each other. They were bolted to the floor.

"Makes it easier to clean up," explained my friend. "They probably don't have the time or manpower to reposition the chairs after every trip." He sat with his back to the bow and I took a chair opposite.

After clearing the breakwater, the ship began to roll, ever so slowly, from side to side. One minute I could see the horizon out the right-hand window, and the next minute there was nothing but sky. My clammy hands gripped the armrests, but it wasn't enough to settle my stomach.

"Face forward," said my friend.

That view was no better. I tried to focus on what else he was saying. His lips were moving, but all I could hear was my inner voice shrieking, "*If you're going to puke, for God's sake get to the bathroom!*"

I tried positive self-talk. *It's only an hour and thirty-five minutes across. You can make it. Keeping smiling. As you act, so shall you believe.*

"Excuse me a moment," I said aloud, "I need to use the ladies' room." Without waiting for an answer, I staggered toward the center of the ship, where I prayed I'd find the proper facilities before I embarrassed myself.

I found the snack bar first. *Crackers! Give me crackers! Saltines! Ritz! Cheez-its! Anything!*

The best there was to offer was an egg salad sandwich. Just the *thought* of the smell of egg salad sent my digestive tract into cartwheels. The vending machine at the end of the counter looked slightly more promising: potato chips, corn chips or preservative-laden peanut butter on cheese crackers.

I put a king's ransom in coins into the slot and retrieved a small bag of corn chips, hastily cramming a few of them into my mouth as I located the rest room.

All the stalls were occupied, so I braced myself against the sink counter and kept busy with the corn chips. Suddenly I envisioned the scene if I did throw up. I pictured corn chip-colored sawdust spewing from a chain saw.

With this image in mind, I lunged for the first empty stall. And there I stood, facing the toilet, holding my hair back with one hand and the rest of the chips in the other, prepared for the worst.

But nothing happened.

The ship was momentarily solid as a rock, and my stomach downscaled from the jitterbug to a nice easy waltz.

Fully clothed, I turned around and perched on the

throne, wondering what would happen next. One minute. Then two. I didn't care if there was a line-up clear around the wheelhouse, I wasn't budging until I was sure the nausea had passed. Three minutes. Then four.

The ship slowly, oh so slowly, leaned to the left, then rolled back to the right...then again to the left...the right...the left... I put my head down on my knees.

As if she'd been waiting for me to get into just this position, the ship suddenly lurched to the right. Water from the toilet slapped the seat of my slacks. I closed my eyes, pursed my lips and held my breath.

The ship pitched left. The stall door, which in my haste I had not secured, soundly smacked the top of my head.

Sometime later, as we entered Victoria's sheltered harbor, I rejoined my companion. My sweater was tied around my waist to hide my wet bottom. I pressed a plastic sandwich bag full of crushed ice against the lump on my forehead.

My friend's brow furrowed with genuine concern. "Are you all right?"

"Of course," I replied. "A piece of cake. Nobody gets seasick on a ship this size."

Public Enemy #1

So there I was, relaxing on the boardwalk in the late afternoon sunshine, minding my own business and sipping a soft drink.

Okay, okay. When I'm armed with my trusty notepad (*which I am rarely without, and usually regret it when I am*) I'm probably not really minding my own business. Everybody else's business seems so much more fun to mind. Eavesdropping is a favorite pastime of mine, and jotting down snippets of overheard conversation is harmless enough. I've never considered that I might pose a threat to society by doing this.

Until now.

On this particular afternoon-turning-evening, only a few hardier souls ventured along the half mile trek to wait for the sunset. It was bright out, but there was a slight chill to the air. I sat backwards at a strategically located picnic table, using the tabletop as a backrest. The perpetual fog bank hovered just offshore, promising some extra color and variety to the twilight display.

I was told when I moved here nearly two decades ago that eventually I'd go weeks and then months without looking out at the ocean. "That's when you'll know you're a local," they said. I've never given much credibility to what they say. In my experience, *they* often don't know their shortbread from a clam donut.

(*Don't ask me what that means—I overheard it in*

the bakery a few weeks ago, scribbled it on the side of my pastry sack, and thought now might be a good time to use it.)

But back to the particular day in question. I had along all the necessities: notepad, pen, diet Pepsi and camera. I'd taken the camera with me in case the sunset was unlike any of the hundreds I'd photographed before. You never know.

Several groups of "I bet I can swing my arms higher than you can" power walkers hot-footed it by. There were a number of couples taking their evening constitutional, some with pets in tow. A few kids (*defined as anyone under the age of 30*) sauntered by in their NBA and NFL attire. A few wannabe kids (*anyone over 30, but faking it*) jogged through in florescent spandex. And then along came Gladys and Henry.

At least I think it was Gladys and Henry. It could have been Mabel and Albert. Or Flossie and Bertram. Or Pearl and Ernie. Whatever. I'm sure if you've frequented the boardwalk you've seen them. They're from Iowa. Or South Dakota. Or Minnesota. Or Kansas. Or someplace like that.

Anyway, Gladys and Henry must have left their hearing aids in the motel, because they were communicating in voices I couldn't help but overhear, even if I hadn't wanted to.

"I don't know why you wanted to get out of the car," said Gladys. "We could see perfectly well where we were. I just hope I don't catch my death of cold out here."

"I thought it'd be nice to get a picture of the ocean to send to the kids," said Henry. "Stand over by railing there. I want you in this."

I stood up and walked toward them. "Excuse me...but if you'd like, I can take the picture for you so you both can be in it…"

Gladys clutched her pocketbook tight to her chest. (*Women like Gladys always carry a pocketbook, and never refer to it as a purse. It's usually no-nonsense black, two-handled and has one heavy-duty metal fastener that snaps shut with a resounding click.*) She looked frantically right and left.

"It's okay," I tried to assure her. "I already *have* a camera." I pointed to the picnic table. "And I can't outrun you." I showed her the brace on my ankle. "I'm just trying to be helpful."

Henry shrugged apologetically. "My wife don't cotton to strangers," he said, showing me the shutter button.

"I live here," I replied. "That kind of makes you guys the strangers, don't you think?" I smiled my most disarming smile.

Henry managed a weak chuckle, but Gladys remained steadfastly unconvinced that my intentions were honorable. I'm afraid the picture I took will reflect that.

Through the viewfinder Gladys was recorded for posterity standing on the boardwalk in a beautiful spring sunset using both hands to clasp her arctic coat around her in a death grip. The expression on her face makes Janet Reno look like Cinderella's fairy godmother.

Henry, shirtsleeves flapping in the breeze, stands next to her looking a might bit perplexed.

Henry, dear soul, is holding the pocketbook.

A Separate Peace

My friend Lee lives in Beavercreek, Oregon. You have to go some to find Beavercreek on a map. You have to go some to find it in your car, too.

Beavercreek, for those with a penchant for geographical knowledge, is about 30 miles south and a little east of downtown Portland. That's probably what makes it seem like another planet.

One minute you're immersed in the most godforsaken tangle of traffic this side of Seattle. The convergence of I-5, I-205, and alternate highway 217, with their multi-lane arrows and exit onlys to Tigard, Tualatin, Beaverton, Sherwood, Salem, West Linn, Lake Oswego, Oregon City, and a dozen more places you'd rather not get confused by, is enough to make you want to hustle right back to our beautiful beach and bury your head in the sand forever.

The next minute you find yourself in a wonderland of green dappled hills, lush deciduous trees, and a quiet so reverent you'd think you'd gone deaf were it not for the unobtrusive chirping of a dozen different species of birds.

"You only make four or five turns after you leave the city," said Lee, giving me directions over the phone, "but there's four to eight miles between each turn."

I met Lee in February. Capitalizing on the technological tools at our disposal, we became cyberspace pen pals, e-mailing each other once or twice a week for the past five months. There's an awful lot you can learn about a person by exchanging that many letters.

Lee's a journeyman carpenter. He designs and constructs high-quality furniture from a variety of hardwoods in a solar heated workshop he built himself. He also writes poetry, plays guitar, rides a mountain bike, trout fishes with flies he ties himself, is an avid bird-watcher, and keeps his Spanish fluent through frequent travels to Mexico.

"I've really been getting into gardening this year," he wrote this spring. "I've dug out several flower beds, and I've designed a grape arbor I want to build out by my long-neglected orchard. I'm planting Irish moss between the stepping-stones I set in the walkway."

"Send some pictures," I wrote back. "I need a visual on this."

His e-mail response caught me by surprise. "Why don't you come see it for yourself?"

A road trip? The idea had immediate appeal, but... *but what*? There was really no reason *not* to go for a visit. I had, as they say, the time, opportunity, and motive... *So why not?*

When I arrived, Lee handed me a glass of iced tea, and we strolled around the property. I was amazed by the deep red-orange color of the earth, in strong contrast to my personal backyard sandscape. We paused in the garden to pick and eat a few raspberries. "This is great," I said. "I'm glad I chose such a nice warm day to see your place."

"It's summer," said Lee, smiling. "Don't forget you're inland now; it's like this almost every day."

"Maybe I've been holed up in the land of fog and drizzle too long," I said. "Two days in a row this hot at the beach would be considered a major heat wave."

Continuing on, Lee stopped momentarily to smell the Sweet Williams growing beneath the rhododendrons and told me the names of various bedding plants along the drive. "And this," he said, pointing to a multitude of tiny green starts carefully inserted among the walkway stones, "is—

"Irish moss!" I interrupted him. "Live and in person!"

He laughed. "I'm beginning to sound like a born-again gardener, aren't I? I've just never been much into landscaping or yard work before. Now I can't wait to get out here and dig around in the dirt whenever I get the chance. Maybe I enjoy it so much because it's new to me."

"Maybe." I nodded, thinking of how the blackberry brambles and salal have devoured many of my rhododendrons and are threatening to reclaim a major portion of my once-cleared yard. "Or maybe you just want to hack out a little corner of the wilderness for your own. Put some order into the natural beauty of the place."

We sat in companionable silence and watched the late afternoon sunlight dance among the trees in the ravine behind his house. Occasionally, I could hear a car pass on the road some distance away.

"What are you smiling about?" asked Lee.

"I was just thinking," I replied, "that to describe this kind of peace by e-mail, you'd have to forward me a blank page." I sighed deeply. "And even that wouldn't do it justice."

Lee said nothing; there was no need for words.

CHAPTER THREE
Unforgettable Characters

Dr. Hook is Alive and Well

"You saw *who* while you were in Nevada?" asked Anna Marie.

"Dr. Hook."

"He isn't, by chance, an orthopedic surgeon, is he?"

I ignored her smirk. "Dr. Hook," I said, feigning exasperation, "otherwise known as Ray Sawyer, was performing at Cactus Pete's casino in Jackpot. Surely you're old enough to remember Dr. Hook!"

"Refresh my memory," said a dubious Anna Marie.

"Dr. Hook and the Medicine Show. Lead guy had a hat curled up on the sides. Wore an eye patch. Early 70s."

"Jan," sighed Anna Marie, "I started *kindergarten* in 1970."

"Okay, so you were practically a babe in arms, but you must have heard his music…"

"Give me some examples."

"'You Make My Pants Want to Get Up and Dance,' 'When You're in Love with a Beautiful Woman,' 'She was Only Sixteen,' "Sharing the Night Together,' 'On the Cover of the Rolling Stone…'

Anna Marie shook her head. "And you say this was

good music?"

"Good music? It was the best! Dr. Hook, in my estimation, was by far the best rock and roll band to come out of the 70s!"

"I thought the 70's contribution to music was disco," said Anna Marie.

"Oh, *pull-eeze*," I choked out, "spare me the sarcasm!"

Dr. Hook's first single, 'Sylvia's Mother,' had topped the charts in 1970. I graduated from high school in 1972. Song lyrics impressed on my memory 'way back then' can still be recalled, with a fair degree of accuracy, after hearing just a few short guitar chords.

Sitting less than 30 feet from the stage, I scanned the audience for a general sense of demographics. Most of us were in our 40s. There were a few groups of younger people, and a handful of senior citizens who, I assumed, got show tickets as part of their hotel package.

The lights dimmed, the curtain went up, and suddenly there he was: the same hat, the same eye patch, the same craggy, character-lined face. From his snakeskin cowboy boots to his ever-present cigarette, Dr. Hook exuded showmanship of the 70s. He didn't just rule the stage—for an hour and a quarter, Dr. Hook ruled the universe.

I was 17 again. I bounced happily in my chair, clapped to the music, and sang along. All around me, dancing eyes and smiling faces reflected my own unbridled joy. Heck, we were all 17 again.

In a trance-like state, I left the show lounge, not ready for the particular noise, excitement and flashing lights of the main gaming room. Retreating to the relative quiet of the hotel café, I ordered a sandwich and a cup of decaf.

My body and brain returned, regretfully, to the

present. I wondered if 'Dr. Hook' had any trouble transforming into 'Ray Sawyer' after his final show of the night. I couldn't imagine him hanging up his hat, changing into his jammies, and watching a bit of Letterman before turning in.

Methodically, I began walking up and down the rows of slot machines in the casino. It was a long shot, but maybe…

And suddenly, there he was: the same hat, the same eye patch, the same craggy, character-lined face. Except now he was a whole lot shorter.

"I got his autograph," I said to Anna Marie. "I'd like to say we had a long, in-depth conversation about the state of rock and roll music in the 90s, but that would be stretching it a bit." I smiled at the memory.

Anna Marie smiled back. "What *did* you say to him?" she prompted.

"I invited him to Grannie Annie's in Ocean Park. I told him we'd play '3801' on the jukebox and sing a duet."

"Thirty-eight-oh-one?"

"Sylvia's Mother." I laughed. "I even confided that 'Sylvia' had been my first computer password."

Anna Marie giggled. "And what did he say about that?"

"He said I was sweet, and when he handed me back my pen, he kissed my hand—right there," I said, pointing.

"And you haven't washed your hands since, right?"

"Don't be ridiculous. Of course I've washed my hands." A slow blush crept up my neck. "But I put the autograph and ticket stub into my scrapbook right away."

"And dusted off your old record albums?" she queried.

"No," I admitted, "I don't own a turntable anymore, and I don't have any Dr. Hook CDs. This is the new millennium, you know."

"I know," said Anna Marie, "but I thought you'd forgotten."

For an hour and a quarter, I had.

Josephine

Crossing the Strait of Georgia from Powell River, British Columbia to Vancouver Island takes a couple hours. A couple hours is usually ample time to have meaningless conversations with several dozen other ferry passengers. Unless, I discovered, the first person you happen to run into is Josephine.

At all of five feet two inches tall, Josephine could have gotten lost in the shadow of her pocketbook. She wore a tailored gray pantsuit accented with a royal blue silk scarf. Jewelry sparkled on every finger; I had no doubt her diamond earrings were real.

"I've come all the way from Wisconsin in a motor coach," she said, nodding toward the mammoth silver tour bus. "Next vacation I'm taking a cruise. At least on a cruise you get to walk around and stretch your legs.

"I don't know why my husband insisted that he wanted to 'see Canada,'" she continued. "As soon as we arrive at our hotel each evening he kicks off his shoes, turns on the TV and sprawls across the bed to watch the news. You call that a vacation? He does the very same thing at home."

I smiled sympathetically and settled in on the bench next to her. By the time we docked in Comox, our plans were set.

Josephine was waiting in the hotel lobby at eight. "You sure you're up for this?" I asked as I helped her fasten the seat belt.

"I'm ready for anything," she crowed. "Let the old fogies turn in early, this gal's looking for adventure!"

"What kind of 'adventure' did you have in mind?"

"Well," she began, her blue eyes mischievous, "I picked up a tourist guide at the restaurant where we had dinner." She dug into her purse and produced the brochure. "Think you can find this address?" She pointed to an ad.

"Josephine!" I laughingly admonished her, "that's a single's bar!"

"Right you are, Honey," she grinned. "We're both over 21 and you're single, so I figure we're a shoo-in."

I turned the car toward the downtown area. "Josephine," I asked a few minutes later, "*Just how old are you?*"

"Not that it's any of your business," she said as she checked her hair in the visor mirror, "but I'll be 79 in a few weeks."

The lighting in the bar left a lot to be desired. Undaunted, Josephine took me by the elbow and led me to an empty table. "Scotch," she told the waitress. Upon seeing my eyebrows ricochet off my hairline, she amended her order. "Make that TWO, on the rocks."

Josephine took advantage of my muted state to scour the room. "There's two possibles right behind you."

"Possible what?" I squeaked out.

"Young man!" Josephine called out over my shoulder. "You and your friend there—why don't you come on over and keep us gals company?"

The table was not big enough for me to crawl under. "Josephine," I whispered, "just what do you think you're doing?"

"I thought you wanted to meet some guys," she whispered back as she pulled an extra chair up to our table.

"Come on," she motioned to the hesitant men, "here's a place for you to sit." The men in question picked up their drinks and dutifully did as they were told.

Josephine asked them their names and introduced herself. "And I'm Sylvia," I quickly interjected.

"That's funny," said Josephine, "I could have sworn you told me your name was JAN…" As my red face heated the room she turned back to the men, "Do you guys dance?"

"There's no band tonight," one of them replied.

"Well there's a jukebox, isn't there?"

Two hours and many dances later, I caught Josephine's attention. "It's nearly midnight…are you getting tired?"

"Tired? Honey, I'm just getting my second wind." She lowered her voice, "And I told my husband not to wait up." Eyeing me suspiciously, she continued, "Unless, of course, *you* want to go…"

I returned Josephine to her hotel a few minutes after the bar closed. The evening's 'adventure' had turned out to be a truly memorable experience, much more fun than if I had ventured out without this dynamo senior citizen activities coordinator.

As we said our goodbyes, Josephine reached over and squeezed my hand. "I had a great time, Honey," she said, "but now I've a confession to make. …I don't think I could live with myself if I let you go on believing I'm 78. Truth is, Honey…truth is, week after next I'll be 82."

Who was that Masked Man?

I reveled in the few minutes of peace and quiet I stole from my busy schedule to sit and meditate on the Seaview beach approach. The windows were all rolled down, allowing a soft breeze to waft through the car.

I glanced casually in my rearview mirror. A shiny black automobile was making its way slowly, oh so slowly, down the potholed road. It might have been one of those Trans Am/Firebird models, or maybe a Camaro—I was never one for details. But I could tell by its older gold-on-blue license plate that it hailed from California.

Curious, I continued to watch as the car came to a stop a hundred or so feet behind me. The driver's door opened, and a long pair of jean-clad legs stepped out. The legs were attached to a handsome man wearing a white scoop neck T-shirt under an open black leather jacket. Make that a VERY handsome man.

He closed the car door and leaned casually against the front fender of his vehicle. Even from this distance I could see his chiseled cheekbones, the angular line of his jaw, his dark brooding eyes. I openly stared, still looking in the rearview mirror, at the way his long black hair ruffled gently in the wind. I felt my pulse accelerate.

Whoa girl, get a grip! I thought, pulling myself abruptly back from a blossoming fantasy. *You've never in your life been attracted to a man with long hair.*

Liar, said my conscience. *Have you forgotten*

Lorenzo Lamas? Branscombe Richmond? Fabio?

Okay, I admit it, maybe once or twice a guy with long hair had turned my head, but this guy was no movie star or romance novel cover model. *Or was he?* After all, his license plate said California…

I leaned forward and twisted the ignition key. I maneuvered a hasty three-point turn, and forcing what I hoped would be mistaken for nonchalance, drove back up the approach. Pulling even with him, I pressed the button to lower my already open window.

Slightly flustered, I nevertheless gave him my biggest, warmest, very best smile. "What part of California are you from?" I queried.

The potential movie star replied that he was from Santa something. I missed most of his response due to the simple fact that he had a voice to match the body. The term 'like honey on toast' came to mind.

"A lot of Californians seem to be migrating to Washington state," I continued. "Are you visiting or have you moved here?" So much for subtlety.

"Both," he answered. "I live in Washington now but I'm here at the coast visiting friends."

For maybe the third time in recorded history, I became suddenly shy. "I hope you enjoy your stay," I mumbled, willing myself to break eye contact.

"Thank you." He smiled again. "And thank you for stopping to say 'hello.'"

I merely nodded and drove numbly on up the road. By the time I reached the highway I was kicking herself for not thinking to ask his name. That was very out of character—I always ask a person's name. But this time, when it might have really counted for something, I'd been struck dumb. *Dumb and dumber*, I thought.

Worse yet, my business card, complete with home

telephone number, remained in the purse sitting on the car seat beside me.

Alas! I lamented, another missed opportunity.

Opportunity for what? said my little inner voice. *You got exactly what you needed—a silly little summer flirtation—what could be better?*

But I didn't want to listen to my little inner voice. What I wanted was to spend some quality time with this mystery man. So what if movie stars and book cover models aren't real? So what if their sole purpose is to inspire a few hours of escapism, a bit of harmless daydreaming? Who's to say a chance encounter on the beach can't develop into something meaningful?

For many months I spent all my spare time out on the Seaview approach gazing longingly into the rearview mirror. (Hindsight is, after all, 20/20.) Then finally, with deep regret, I realized that lightning rarely strikes twice in the same location. *Besides,* I rationalized with a wry little smile, *if we had driven off into the sunset together, we both would have drowned.*

An insufferable romantic, perhaps I would have recovered sooner if I had bothered to look up the definition of the word 'harlequin.'

Bless Her Heart

Every so often I miss Aunt Flora. She was my great aunt actually, my grandfather's sister. Aunt Flora, affectionately called 'A.F.', lived till she was just a month short of her 98th birthday.

I don't remember her as a young woman; she was already well into her sixties when I was born. Neither do I remember ever having seen a picture of her when her wispy hair was darker than a blue-tinged white, tucked into a feathery roll on the back of her head.

For the first 18 or 20 years of my life, Aunt Flora sent me two dollars for my birthday. Two one dollar bills, rumpled and wadded and folded again and again before they were tucked inside a generic little greeting card, the kind of all-occasion card that came 20 to a box.

I'd be willing to bet that even with all her nieces and nephews she never used up a whole box of those cards. Waste not, want not, Aunt Flora was one of the world's first recyclers.

Armed with a sharp pair of pinking shears, A.F. trimmed off the signature inside the cards she received, signed her name above the scalloped edge, and mailed the card back out when the next occasion arose.

Many times Mother and I laughed ourselves silly over the creative ways she cut out the entire center of the older-style, multi-paged folded cards, sometimes totally obliterating the original verse. Then, in her trademark shaky scrawl, she'd pen in a greeting of her own.

Even the envelopes could be reused. A.F. figured out a nifty way to turn them inside-out using the eraser end of a pencil. A little glue sealed the envelope shut—good as new.

Aunt Flora was frugal to a fault. When I graduated from high school, she slipped me five dollars (all folded and creased one dollar bills) when Uncle Jay wasn't looking and told me to keep mum about it. Later Gramps told me to go buy myself a new watch for graduation and pulled some money from his wallet.

Old Eagle Eye stepped swiftly forward. "Charlie!" Aunt Flora whispered urgently, grabbing at his wrist. He held out what looked to me like a 20-dollar bill. "Charlie! Charlie! There's *two* there Charlie! There's *two* there! That's *forty dollars* Charlie!"

Now that I think about it, that was right about the time I stopped getting any money in my birthday cards from A.F. Guess she thought I'd outgrown the tradition.

But one tradition steadfastly remains. Whenever Mom or I receive an especially funny card, or one with a great picture or poignant message we want to pass on, out come the pinking shears. Only these days we both sign our 'used' cards with the initials 'A.F' in fond remembrance.

Aunt Flora's legacy includes rules for small town gossiping. "You can say prittin'near anything about anybody as long as you bless their heart," she told me. "That way they know you don't mean no harm by it." Then she'd look around to see who was listening before repeating the juicy news of the day.

"You know Mrs. Taylor's daughter Rachel? She's a wild one, bless her heart. That girl's going to be getting herself in the family way if she keeps a-carrying on with that Andrews boy…

"And have you heard about Mr. Walker? Why I hear

tell he drinks till he can't rightly stand up nearly every evening, bless his heart...

"Surely you remember old man Patterson, down at the market? Well! Mrs. Snyder swears she saw him putting his thumb down, bless his heart, on the meat scale while he was weighing up her pork chops."

Years later, whenever I catch myself saying something none-too-kind about another human being, I quickly check my tongue and end my tirade by reciting A.F.'s three-word absolution.

I don't know why Aunt Flora's been on mind so much lately. Memories are tricky things. Maybe it was the smell of lilacs and wisteria blooming
in the yard that set me to reminiscing. Could've been the hymns we sang last week in church; A.F. was always humming hymns. Perhaps it was as simple as seeing a two-pocketed blue gingham apron trimmed with white rick-rack hanging on display in a local antique shop.

They say that memories, like wine, get better with age. Now that's a thought that would've gotten a swift rise out of A.F. Aunt Flora was a former president of her local chapter of the Women's Christian Temperance Union, bless her heart.

Yes, every so often, I miss Aunt Flora.

You Can't Teach a Dead Dog New Tricks

I could attempt to give her anonymity by using a fictitious name, but I don't think I could fool anybody. There's way too many folks around here who will be able to attribute the classic malapropism I used for the title of this column in less time than it takes to read this sentence.

Miriam said it.

And during her eight-year residence on the peninsula, Miriam also taught us that there's no sense crying over slow molasses, and that it's always darkest just before you leap.

There's a lot of wisdom in those words; Miriam is one smart woman.

Miriam, who taught public school for twenty-something years, retired last June. Or so we thought. To retire, by definition, means to withdraw from action or danger; to retreat, fall back, or remove one's self from usual use or service. (*I've also heard it said that to "retire" is to get four new radials and go another 40,000 miles.*)

According to the letter I received last Saturday, Miriam never considered retiring in the traditional sense of the word. It looks to me like she's just shifting gears.

The manila envelope was postmarked Washington D.C. and "for official government use only" was printed in the return address corner. It was from the Peace Corps. Would I mind answering a few questions about Miriam?

I dropped everything to tell them what I knew—after all, this was the *Government* asking. Far be it from me to delay, even for a few hours, a governmental request of this nature just a handful of weeks prior to the ominous April 15th! One can never be too careful!

But what started out as a simple task of marking appropriate boxes, circling a few numbers, and filling in the blanks, soon escalated into a medium-sized dissertation. How could I adequately describe her boundless energy, unbridled enthusiasm, and incessant verve and gusto for life without elaborating in the "additional comments" section? To say merely that she taught junior high math and science, grades 1, 2 and 3 (*some years at the same time*), revitalized the church youth group, and sponsored dozens of foster children, still didn't seem to convey the deep commitment she has for doing her part to make the world a better place.

My reference letter began to sound a lot like a eulogy—and at first that made me extremely uncomfortable. So I dug out "Mr. Webster" again and discovered that a eulogy was precisely what I wanted it to sound like. Eulogies are not reserved exclusively for funerals; eulogies are a commendatory formal statement, spoken or written, of high praise, specifically to extol a person's character, accomplishments, etc.

And Miriam certainly deserves a eulogy. She is an inspiration to everyone who comes into contact with her. She is a friend, a mentor, and a role model. For her to choose to head overseas, into unknown and most likely primitive living conditions, all the while pushing darn close to sixty, well, that's an illustration I'll proudly to hold up to today's youth.

At an age when a lot of adults begin to slow down and take things a little easier, Miriam goes out and reminds us that we all have plenty to give, that we have talents to share, and that caring about others knows no age boundary. No, Miriam's not a retired teacher; today she's teaching each of us a little more about selflessness. Let's hope we're good students.

And while it's true that you can't teach a dead dog new tricks, it's nice to have someone around like Miriam to point out that mature individuals are still quite capable of forging ahead, avoiding complacency, and of seeking out and conquering an endless supply of challenges.

I was delighted to write the Peace Corps a glowing reference letter for Miriam. She is a fine example of continuing to reach for the brass carrot dangling at the end of the tunnel.

What I Should Have Told Him

I imagine the family received hundreds of letters. Maybe even thousands. Many others probably thought about writing, or at least sending a card, but didn't get around to it.

I almost didn't get around to it myself. I spent four long hours at the keyboard, agonizing over each word, before I was satisfied with what little I composed. Letters of condolence aren't my strong suit.

Don Smith, better known as Chief Lelooska, passed away a few weeks ago. He was a Cherokee by birth, a Kwakiutl by adoption. He spent most of his life as an artist and an educator of north coast Indian lore. And although he wouldn't have been able to place my name with my face, I considered him my mentor, my friend.

I became acquainted with the Lelooska Foundation in the early '80s while on a field trip with my third grade class. Along with hundreds of elementary students from dozens of other area schools, we filed quietly into a cold, dark longhouse in Ariel, Washington.

Rows of bleacher-type benches lined the side walls. The pungent odor of cedar mingled with the scent of the heavily-trodden earth floor. In the center of the room a fire was set, but not lit. At the far end of the longhouse was a white fur-covered bench flanked by large carvings of mysterious totem figures.

As we huddled close for warmth, white feathers and

fluff spewed from the mouth of one carved statue, the Tsonoqua, followed by eerie whistling noises and words in a language I did not understand.

A masked woman danced into the room. She was wrapped in a red and blue button blanket. Her carved headdress exaggerated human features in garish colors. She gracefully swayed and chanted while moving around the center ring, always to the right.

First smoke, and then flame, billowed forth. The children sat in awed silence as the flickering flames made ghostly patterns on the longhouse walls. Her mission accomplished, the woman danced back behind the partition as Lelooska entered the room.

Lelooska. "To Cut Against Wood With a Knife." Master storyteller, carver, and keeper of the culture. He told us tales of creation, why the salmon return to the same stream each year, and how the sisters, Half Moon and Full Moon, battled over possession of the night sky. In less than an hour, I was hooked.

With Lelooska as a guiding force, I expanded my knowledge of the north coast Indian culture in leaps and bounds. I took university classes on-site at the foundation, read numerous books, travelled to dozens of museums.

I've observed Kwakiutl carvings from Alert Bay, off the northern tip of Vancouver Island, to the display featuring one of Lelooska's totem poles in the Denver Museum of Natural History. Sitting on the beach at Cape Mudge on Quadra Island, I wrote poetry about its first inhabitants. I am proud to be a card-carrying member of the Nuyumbalees Society at the Kwakiutl museum at Quathkiaski Cove.

My bookshelves hold over 50 tomes on the subject of north coast Indian art, history, legends and personalities. The walls of my home office are covered in prints of

Kwakiutl design. But my pride and joy is a small collection of miniature totem poles.

Granted, most of my totem poles are cheap imitations of authentic carvings. Some are even ceramic and mass-produced. And all of them are what could be referred to as "tourist trinkets." Yet each pole brings back a special memory, representing those places I've visited while learning more about the native coastal peoples.

I never wrote to Lelooska to tell him what an enormous influence he had, and continues to have, on me. I wrote to his family last week, but it's not the same. I regret each time I thought about writing him, but didn't make it a priority. It's too late to tell Lelooska, but it's never really too late.

There are many other people in my present and my past that have meant a great deal to me and the way I live my life. I am compiling a list of those mentors; I will write to them soon—very soon. I shall make it a continuing priority to count my friends as blessings, and I won't hesitate to tell them so.

This is my tribute to Lelooska.

The Old Man and the Ski Lift

Many writers are, for the most part, well-adjusted and happy with their lot in life. Others are loners, abuse alcohol, and wander aimlessly through a myriad of unsatisfactory relationships.

I consider myself among the first group. Hemingway, London, Crane, Steinbeck and Poe obviously belong to the second group. (It may be noted here that not many in the first category make the best-seller list, but we have a propensity to live a bit longer.) Yet in some strange way, all writers are cut from the same cloth—inextricably connected.

A few of my closest friends know of my imagined affinity with Ernest Hemingway.

Terry knows. He sent me a postcard from Sloppy Joe's Bar in Key West, Florida and brought me a paper drink coaster from there with Papa's picture on it.

Shelia knows. She witnessed my royal blue funk after we saw "Love and War," the movie about Hemingway's first love and misdirected pride.

And Steve knows. He watched me trudge ten miles through snowdrifts six feet deep to visit the Hemingway memorial on the banks of Trail Creek in Sun Valley, Idaho.

Okay, maybe it was only a little over a quarter mile from where we parked the van, and maybe the snow was only a foot and a half deep, but the going was treacherous—especially with a cartilage-free left knee and a right Achilles tendon held together by nothing more than surgeon's sutures.

"Whose crazy idea was this?" I panted, extracting my leg from yet another sinkhole.

"I'm pretty sure it was yours," said Steve.

"Do you think the ambulance will be able to reach us, or will I have take the life-flight out of here?" I asked, crashing down through the crusty snowpack a fourth or fifth time.

Steve clicked the camera shutter in my direction but did not respond.

I stayed on my rear end and slid the last 20 feet to the tromped down area in front of the bronze bust perched atop the stone monument. It was not quite the dignified entrance I wanted to make, but it got the job done, and I was still in one piece.

Steve pulled me to my feet and we brushed the snow off the plaque at the base of the monument. I read the words aloud: "Best of all he loved the fall, the leaves yellow on the cottonwoods, leaves floating on the trout streams, and above the hills the high blue windless skies… Now he will be a part of them forever."

I sat back down in the snow, awed by the solemnity of the place, unmindful of the cold creeping into my soul.

"It's a beautiful spot in the summertime," said Steve after a while. "And in the fall the yellow cottonwood leaves make a kind of golden canopy. There's a bench by that retaining wall there that makes a great resting place along the hiking path."

All that was visible of the retaining wall were a few rocks peeking out from a snowdrift. No bench or river trail was apparent.

"I guess I'll have to take your word for it." I smiled, thinking of the fall—October—my favorite month, and another connection to the quintessential wordsmith.

My nearly frozen backside finally got my attention. Rising quietly, I listened to the swiftly moving water beneath the bank. Across the creek a cluster of condos stood out against the bluff. "I wonder what Papa would think of the present-day residents of this valley."

Steve shrugged. "He liked to hunt, he liked to fish, but I don't think he spent much time skiing."

Or did he? Hemingway's picture graces the halls of the Sun Valley Lodge alongside many celebrities of the 40s and 50s. Granted, he's not shown wearing skis in the bar, but you never know.

The cabin where he took his life is on privately owned land not far from the memorial. The Nature Conservancy has taken up residence there, and it is no longer open to the public.

But gazing at the snow-covered hills surrounding Ketchum, I felt the undeniable presence of the man who won the Nobel Prize for literature the year I was born.

"People who have creative talents see the world differently," said Steve, "and because they see the world differently, they tend to be isolated from other people."

Hemingway wrote from that deepest place within himself. With every word, he sought to explain the essence of human existence. Although personal experience has motivated us both, he wrote very little humor. But that dissimilarity doesn't mean I can't receive a Pulitzer…

…or enjoy trout fishing.

CHAPTER FOUR
Diet and Exercise

Just Weight till Next Week

It's D-Day. It's also the day before my birthday. Every year on this day I take time to evaluate the past year, chalk up the pluses and minuses, and vow to discipline myself more rigidly in the year to come.

Discipline is a good D-day word. So is defend, democracy, determination, devotion, dignity, and duty. But for most of us born post-1944, there's one D-word that rises above all others for emotional impact, one word that never fails to fill our modern-day hearts with trepidation.

That word, for those whose morning coffee hasn't yet reached their brain, is 'diet.'

Take a good look at the first three letters of that four-letter word. How can anything be good for you that starts with '*die*'?

I figure some of us are supposed to be fat. If it weren't for us chubby types, the thin ones wouldn't think they looked nearly so good. And if God wanted us all to be thin, She wouldn't have invented white chocolate raspberry cheesecake, now would She?

We've all heard the jokes: "I'm on a seafood diet—I see food, I eat it." "I'm on a food reduction diet—I'm reducing the world's food supply." "I only eat when I'm awake—I can't help it if I'm an insomniac."

We've all heard the excuses: "It's my metabolism." "I'm big-boned." "It's genetic." "I'm under a lot of stress." "I had an unhappy childhood." "It's the medication I'm on." "I'm forced to eat pizza for every meal because my body won't tolerate synthetic vitamins and pizza contains all the major food groups."

But hope springs eternal, and two months ago I decided to check out a newly-formed weight loss support group. This group doesn't advocate any specific diet plan, but requires attendance every week to 'face the music.'

'Facing the music' is not one of my favorite activities. Minutes after the first meeting I found myself at the McDonald's drive-through window. 'One last hurrah' I rationalized. I ordered a bacon cheeseburger, French fries and a DIET pop. Hey, every little bit helps.

Week two I got down to business. I didn't order the French fries. Week three I figured I'd better eat the French fries so I could truthfully check off a 'vegetable' serving on my food chart. Week four I removed my fingernail polish and earrings before weighing in. Week five I shaved my legs.

To make a long story shorter, after eight weeks my net loss is two pounds and 56 days.

One of the organizers of the group, who asked to be called Hillary, is a bouncy blonde 25-year-old with more cheerful energy than a 6-month-old cocker spaniel. To make matters worse, I'm sure she tips the scale within four or five pounds of the exact weight of my left leg.

I like her anyway.

Hillary went over the goals for the group at our last meeting. "You know, Jan," she said, "it's seven months till the end of December. If you really wanted to, you could become our 'queen' this year."

"I...don't...think...so...," I began slowly, not wanting to offend those in the group whose life's ambition rose no higher than being crowned weight-loss queen. I lowered my voice to a mere whisper, "I've never looked especially good in a tiara..."

Another member of the group suggested we participate in a walkathon as a club fundraiser. "We could tie it in with the World's Longest Beach Walk/Run," said a third member. "The best part about that three-mile walk is that they always have yummy cookies and cranberry juice at the end."

I'm sure her heart's in the right place.

Planning to get a little exercise myself, I bought a new swimming suit and got the schedule for water aerobics classes. I modeled the suit for my friend Anna Marie before taking to the water. She took a long, long, look and sighed a long, long, sigh.

"You bought a black and white swimsuit?" she said, observing the obvious. "I don't think I'd be brave enough to wear a black and white suit in public." She shook her head. "Not after I heard that the sequel to 'Free Willy' is going to be filmed here this summer."

It'll probably be a few more weeks before I'm speaking to dear Anna Marie. And like it or not, this'll be another summer I won't be sunning myself on Normandy Beach.

Or anywhere else.

Say "Cheese"

"Since you're going to be in Bellevue anyway," said my friend Anna Marie, "could you possibly stop by Larry's Market and pick up some good Brie for me?"

"Brie?" I asked. "You want me to go shopping in Bellevue for Brie?"

Her head bobbed enthusiastically.

"Then you'll have to give me a hint," I told her. "Is 'Brie' an animal, mineral or vegetable?"

"Oh Jan," she laughed, "you put on such a good act. For a minute you really had me going. I thought maybe you'd never eaten Brie before."

I hadn't.

And so I ventured naively into Larry's Market, a.k.a. The Yuppie Deli Grocery Store From Hell, and threw myself on the mercy of the first clerk I met.

"Cheese is right next to the other dairy products," he informed me.

Cheese! Thank God! Cheese was a familiar word! Cheese comes from cows, or goats, or possibly some other milk-bearing animals, the likes of which I couldn't recall just then. But now I figured I had more than enough knowledge to purchase this Brie stuff.

Unfortunately, the cheese department was larger than many classrooms I've taught in.

I searched my brain for more data. Cheese should be orange or white. If in brick form, it should say 'cheddar,' or 'mozzarella' on the plastic wrapper. If in a green, cylindrical can, it's 'Parmesan.' If it comes in a shiny foil wrapper, it's from Philadelphia. Nothing in my humble white bread and Velveeta background prepared me for the profusion of cheese choices at Larry's.

I perused the multi-layered display cooler from one end to the other. Everywhere were names of cheeses I couldn't pronounce, imported from countries I thought no longer existed. The colors, textures and varieties seemed endless, but I finally managed to locate the Brie.

Ten or twelve brands of Brie.

Okay, since it worked before, I figured I could try pleading ignorance one more time. "Excuse me," I said to the young woman behind the counter, "I need some expert advice. Can you tell me a little about Brie?"

The woman's face fairly glowed as she began what I can only assume was a highly detailed account of the entire Brie-making process, from the special dietary requirements of the cud-chewing bovines to the slicing of the cheese wheel, wrapping the wedges and pricing the finished product right there on her very own cutting board.

I can only *assume* she said this, because her entire discourse was in French.

Either this dairymaid was imported along with the cheese, or I had stumbled upon some smart-aleck third-year French student practicing the fine art of embarrassing uninitiated Brie buyers.

I spoke slowly and carefully, "Just tell me which brand of Brie you think is best."

"Best? You want the best Brie?" she asked with a heavy accent.

I smiled and nodded.

"For that, mademoiselle, you have to go to Europe."

My smile disappeared. "Is there someone else here

who could help me?"

She shrugged and directed me toward another young woman busily cleaning utensils.

"Can you help me pick out a good Brie?" I asked.

"Any one of those is pretty good," she said, using a knife to point to several offerings.

Relieved, I selected a wedge of each of the three types she recommended, thanked her, and turned to leave.

"Wait!" she called. "You want crackers with that?"

I bolted for the nearest check stand. The clerk, trying to be helpful, began explaining about letting the Brie sit at room temperature for several hours before serving. But, he cautioned, on a day like this it might ripen too rapidly in a hot car.

Not wanting to risk having my hard-won trophies spoil on the long trip home, I set the car's air conditioner on maximum and aimed the vents at Anna Marie's precious bag of cheese. By the time I reached the Peninsula, I had nearly frozen my buns off.

But Anna Marie was not at home when I returned; no one knew exactly when she'd be back.

The first day I faithfully guarded the refrigerated cheese. The second day I chiseled a small portion from each wedge—just to check it out. The third day I began wondering how Brie would taste in a grilled sandwich. Fortunately, Anna Marie arrived home on day four.

"You brought me some Brie!" she exclaimed, examining the re-wrapped packages. "And you wanted me to believe you didn't have culture!"

"What I know for sure about *culture*," I said with a straight face, "is that the more you eat it, the more you get."

In the Swim

"One... two... three... four... five... six... seven... eight... Reverse. One... two... three... four... five... six... seven... eight... Change legs. One... two... three... four..."

The routine was familiar; I set my body on automatic pilot and let my mind drift back to the beginning of the summer...

"You're going to do *what*?" asked an incredulous Anna Marie. "Aren't you the one who told me that *exercise* was a four-lettered word?"

"I think I can live with this," I hastened to explain. "In the pool I might not feel like every joint in my body is being bludgeoned with a baseball bat."

"Do you have a swimsuit?" she queried.

"Hold that thought." I set my cup down and left the kitchen to rummage through my closet, my bureau, my suitcase, the laundry hamper...

At long last, I emerged, modeling my pool attire and sucking in my stomach for all I was worth.

Anna Marie looked me up and down. "Turn around," was all she said, although she appeared to be stifling the urge to say a whole lot more.

I winced. "No one will be looking at my backside in the pool—most of the time it'll be under water. Besides, everyone's there to improve his or her own level of fitness."

"Shall I call you Shamu?" asked my (*former*) best

friend.

"Shamu?"

"Shamu, the killer whale...you're wearing a black and white swimsuit."

"I believe the politically correct term is Orca." I made a face at her as I retreated from the room to dress.

"*There she blows!*" Anna Marie got in the last word, but my mind was made up.

And so it was that two months ago I made a commitment to climb out of bed every Monday, Wednesday and Friday morning, pull on my killer whale disguise, grab a towel and head for the pool before my first cup of tea.

Two months. That's eight weeks, three times a week—a total of 24 hours of water aerobics. So what did I prove?

For one thing, there's a terrific sense of accomplishment in finishing what you start. I committed to a short-term exercise program, and I stuck to my plan, come heck or high water. Mostly high water.

"One... two... three... four... five..."

I smiled as my right elbow came in contact with my left knee. Two months ago those specific body parts hadn't come together in years. Two months ago I hadn't been able to reach my right hand over my right shoulder and touch the fingertips of my left hand wrapped around behind my back, either.

While Andrea counted off the repetitions, I sang silently: 'Row, row, row your boat...' 'We all live in a yellow submarine...' 'It's the story, of a lovely lady, who was bringing up three very lovely girls...' *hey, wait just a darn minute! how did the theme from* 'The Brady Bunch' *sneak in there?*" I laughed aloud, swallowed some chlorinated water, and came up sputtering.

A lot of thoughts have time to float through one's mind in an hour of water aerobics: *I've got to get mom's birthday present to the post office before noon; i wonder if Anna Marie can meet me for lunch; how many calories are in a crab salad?*

Anna Marie did meet me for lunch. "So," she said between bites of her French dip sandwich, "you made it. The summer's over. Aren't you glad you don't have to get up and go swimming any more?"

"Glad?" I shook my head. "I met some really nice people at the pool. Sure, I'm ready for the new school year, but I'll miss the organized splashing around first thing in the morning." I took another stab at the lettuce and tomato on my plate and chewed it thoughtfully.

"I'm considering joining the evening exercise class," I continued. "It'll mean rearranging my schedule a bit, and I won't be able to go every Tuesday and Thursday, but I'd like to continue working out on a regular basis."

"I don't believe I'm hearing this," said Anna Marie. "What turned you into such a fitness convert?"

"Maybe I just enjoy the healthy habit of releasing all those happy little endorphins into my system." I took a sip of my iced tea and smiled. "Or maybe it's because I've lost 23 pounds in the last two months."

Anna Marie's eyes flitted from her catsup-smothered French fries to my dressing-free salad. "What time does the evening class begin?"

"See you at six."

Theobroma Cacao

Milton Snaveley had a town in Pennsylvania named after him. You've probably heard of it; his last name was Hershey.

Hershey, Pennsylvania, founded in 1903, is the home of the world's largest chocolate manufacturing plant. Which naturally makes it a mecca for true chocoholics, myself included.

The United States ranks tenth in the world for per capita chocolate consumption: 10 pounds annually. Switzerland is first with 21 pounds per person. Heck, I eat that much of the sweet stuff in less than a month.

How well I remember the day I realized my genetic inclination toward this delightful treat. It was Valentine's Day. I was nine, maybe 10 years old. The four of us kids had chipped in to buy Mom a five-pound box of Brach's Chocolates at the Ben Franklin five and dime.

Later that afternoon I walked into the living room to discover my mother sitting on the edge of the stone fireplace hearth, the mammoth single-layer box open on her lap. With a glazed look in her eyes she was rapidly flinging empty crinkle-cup wrappers onto the floor to the right and the left of her.

"Mother!" I exclaimed. "What are you doing?!"

"These little papers are just slowing me down!" she panted.

I reached for a chocolate treat. She slapped my hand

away. "Did you buy these for me or for you?"

"Come on, Mom," I begged, "we thought you'd share."

"You thought wrong," she said, sticking her teeth into yet another confection.

I slumped onto the sofa across the room from her and tried to look pitiful. It worked.

"Oh, all right," she sighed, tossing me a piece of candy. "You can have this one."

"Uh, Mom? This one has a bite taken out of it."

"You didn't think I'd give you one I *liked*, did you?"

"You *meant* to give me a *used* chocolate?!"

She put her finger to her lips. "Don't tell your siblings, or they'll be wanting one too."

And the rest, as they say, is history. During my teen years I refined my chocolate obsession: Frangos from Frederick and Nelson's, Bavarian chocolates from that cute little chalet in Issaquah, melt-in-your-mouth mint truffles, Betty Crocker brownies, chocolate-covered cherries and walnut fudge.

I memorized the candy diagram in the lid of the Whitman's chocolate box the same year I memorized the preamble to the constitution.

It didn't take me long to figure out that M&M peanuts, while never melting in my hand, contained less chocolate per pound than plain M&Ms.

Hershey's syrup is my favorite pancake garnish, German chocolate cake is a staple for every birthday celebration, and I've been known to consider murder to get my hands on authentic tollhouse cookies.

But the rumor that I once gave a fourth-grade student an A on his math test for a half dozen of those cookies is completely unfounded. (*It was his spelling test, and he usually got an A anyway...*)

While the average American admits to having an occasional sweet tooth craving, I've always been far above average. All 32 of my chompers regularly unite in their own version of the Hallelujah Chorus, compelling me to drive miles out of my way for a waffle cone filled with "Death by Chocolate," my favorite ice cream flavor.

Yet chocolate, ice cream notwithstanding, is considered a "hot" food in contemporary folk medicine. And cold-classified illnesses like arthritis, colds and gastric complaints must be treated with "hot" foods and remedies.

Personally, I find preventive medicine the best type, so I'm actually keeping myself healthy by eating large quantities of the C-word.

Besides, lecithin is found in all living cells, especially in nerve and brain tissue and red blood cells. Processed lecithin is used as an emulsifying agent in the manufacture of chocolate where fats or oils must be mixed with water. Although no clear evidence exists that lecithin protects against heart attacks or other diseases, there's a widespread underground movement that claims otherwise.

They're the same people promoting chocolate as the fifth major food group.

Chocolate allegedly provides a chemical rush to the brain similar to that of falling in love. And chocolate, although blamed for adolescent acne outbreaks, will never break your heart.

So this Valentine's Day, while I'm busy devouring bags of Milton Snaveley's kisses, I'll raise my mug of chocolate in salute to Swedish botanist Carolus Linnaeus, who, in 1728, classified the cacao plant *theobroma cacao*: "food of the gods."

Long Beach Woman Drowns on Boardwalk

I trembled as I imagined the headline. Was hypothermia taking hold? How long before my cold and damp body would be found? Would Steve travel all the way from Idaho to attend my funeral?

Steve. *This was all Steve's fault.* If he hadn't challenged me to walk a mile each day for 30 consecutive days, this never would have happened! With renewed determination I willed myself to place one foot in front of the other.

It was day 21. For the 20 days previous I had traversed, albeit at a less than record-breaking pace, the entire length of our glorious boardwalk—and back. For 20 consecutive days the weather had miraculously cleared by the time I had the opportunity to stroll along the beach. For 20 consecutive days I had remembered to put my tennis shoes, scarf and raincoat into the car each morning so I'd be ready to hit the planks right after work.

But not this particular morning.

This particular morning I foolishly decided it might be fun to walk *before* work. At home I laced up my tennies, tied back my hair and completely forgot about throwing the raincoat anywhere near the car.

Not -to-worry, I told myself when I realized I was sans my trusty duck suit, *you haven't even been sprinkled on in the past 20 days—why should number 21 be any different?*

I felt noble as all get-out just thinking about my venture. *I'll reward myself with a latté when I'm finished walking. Even better, I'll have today's exercise all out of the way.*

But as pride goeth before a fall, so does smugness preclude sure catastrophe.

I took stock of the cloud formations as I arrived at the 10th Street approach. There were a few nasty-looking portions of sky just off North Head. According to the flags I observed while driving through town, the wind was due west. *I'll be back in less than 20 minutes*, I reasoned, *I can make it.*

I parked the car, zipped up my light weight windbreaker and pulled back on the door handle. The door didn't open. Apparently the wind was blowing a teensy bit harder than first estimated.

At this point any sane person would have recognized an omen, but no, I was hell-bent on continuing my odyssey. I shoved with both hands against the car door and managed to get my left leg wedged between the door and the frame. Using my calf as a lever, I extracted my body from the automobile.

Okay, I thought, *so it'll take me a little longer to walk against this headwind. But the boardwalk's dry, and I'm already here, so I may as well get trekking.*

The half-mile trip north was uneventful. Even lonely. No other walkers braved the elements. *Ha*! I gloated. *I won't let a little wind stop me!*

I tagged the far end of the railing and turned back. *It's downhill from here,* I smiled, *I'm half-way home.*

No sooner did the thought cross my consciousness than the sky opened. Buckets and buckets and buckets of icy rain washed over my head, down my collar and through my pant legs. My glasses fogged up. My hair clung in stringy rivulets to frozen cheeks. Here I was, the unexpected winner of a wet T-shirt contest, and I was half a mile, minus two steps, from the car.

The choices were simple: I could curl up right there and die, or I could call upon the strength of visualizing the sweet revenge I'd have on Steve—somehow, somewhere, someday…

Obviously, since I lived to tell the story, I made it back to the car. I even stopped for my latté on the way to work. But there was no time to go home for a change of clothes.

My compassionate colleagues came to the rescue. Their compassion, plus two space heaters, one hair dryer, a towel, a borrowed pair of socks, and in less than a quarter hour, I was nearly good as new. Of course, I had to suffer the jokes about being wet behind the ears (and everywhere else), and the rumor went 'round that I had put my bra in the microwave to dry it out, but all in all, the teasing wasn't too bad.

That was day 21. Today is day 32—thirty-*two*; Steve owes me *Big time*. I think tonight I'll "reach out and touch someone." I tremble as I imagine the headline: *Idaho man strangled with long distance phone lines.*

Perfect!

Close Encounters of the Culinary Kind

The Secret Caesar Salad Society of Seaview convened at my home shortly after seven-thirty.

"I don't think this is a legal meeting," accused Googie. "You live in Long Beach."

"Yes, but don't forget that the orginal purpose of tonight's get-together was so we all could watch 'Harold and Maude,'" I reminded her. "And since I've got the biggest house, we agreed to meet here."

"I guess it's okay," she conceded, "since we're also having my famous chicken and cream cheese enchiladas. But if the main event was Caesar salad, I think we'd still have to meet in Seaview."

I agreed with her in theory, yet I wasn't about to pass up a chance to dine on her husband's recipe for the world's greatest Caesar salad, even though hubby and son wouldn't be returning from business in Seattle until sometime later in the evening.

"Don't worry," said Googie. "Lavida can make the salad. She knows all the secret ingredients."

So a little after eight, Googie's daughter Lavida and her friend B.B. took over my kitchen to finish preparing dinner while I popped the video into the VCR.

'Harold and Maude' was one of the classic movies of the early 1970s. But somehow I'd missed it. In a moment of weakness, I admitted to Googie that this was yet another embarrassing gap in my cultural education. "I must have been distracted by college," I confessed.

So there I sat, surrounded by friends who were all busier watching my reaction to the movie than the movie itself, when the action suddenly switched to the kitchen.

"Oh no," I heard B.B. exclaim, "Lavida's set the oven on fire!"

My head swiveled in that direction. From the rec room I had a clear view. B.B. wasn't kidding. Orange flames leapt the height of the oven. Smoke billowed into the room.

"Close the oven door," I called, but I never moved. *I never moved.* I just sat there, transfixed by abject terror, while another friend bolted into the kitchen, grabbed the box of baking soda, flung the contents into the oven and slammed the door tight.

The fire went out in seconds; the smoke took quite a bit longer to clear.

"You were *so calm*," said Googie.

Calm? She thought I was *calm?* It's amazing what happens during a massive adrenalin rush. First, I realized that no one in the house but me could give accurate directions to the fire department. Then I wondered if my cat was in or out. Next I wondered why I keep my back-up computer files in the same room as the originals. I wondered what we'd eventually have for dinner. I wondered if my insurance would be cancelled. I wondered if I could get my car out of the garage before the whole place became a blazing inferno. I wondered where my car keys were.

All this flashed through my mind in less time than it takes for a single heartbeat.

"There was no need to panic," I lied. "I figured one of you guys would take care of it. And I promised to stay out of the kitchen tonight, remember? Besides, there's a fire extinguisher in the cupboard next to the refrigerator. If I'd thought things were truly out of control, you'd have seen me move, all right."

I wondered if that was true.

"The only thing you did," said Googie, shaking her head, "was push 'pause' on the remote control. I've never seen anyone so calm."

A short time later we sat down to dinner. "So what actually happened?" I asked nonchalantly.

"I'm so embarrassed," said Lavida. "When the grated cheese melted on top of the enchiladas, the cream in the casserole dish overflowed." Her face turned a deep pink. "You'll probably never invite me over again."

"Of course I will," I consoled her. "Now I've got something to write for next week's column."

Raucous laughter and obvious relief encircled the table. The phone rang. "We're back," said Googie's husband. "Is there any salad left?"

"Salad we've got," I reported. "We even saved you some Chicken Enchiladas Flambé, if you hurry."

"Some what?"

"There was a slight change of menu," I explained. "Lavida decided to barbecue the main dish, but it still tastes great."

"Is everyone okay?"

"We're having a grand time," I replied honestly. "We took a break for dinner, but if you come right over you can catch the last part of the movie with us."

I hung up the phone and dug out my grocery list. In bold letters I wrote 'baking soda' at the top.

The Exercist

"What's all this stuff?" asked Anna Marie, helping me carry numerous packages from the car to the house.

"My mail."

She raised an eyebrow. "Something tells me I'm transporting quite a bit more than an ordinary day's correspondence."

"Okay, okay, I tell you...there's really no need to badger me." I laughed as I dumped the last load on the rec room floor. "It's a new exercise program."

Now it was Anna Marie's turn to laugh. "Who's it for?"

Exercise, long thought to be an eight letter four-lettered word, is one of the top three New Year's resolutions made by the less-than-svelte American populace. It ranks right up there with "lose weight" and "save money." Unfortunately, to lose weight and exercise, one often has to abandon any thought of conserving one's finances. Fitness costs big bucks.

Commercial diet programs usually have an enrollment fee, dues, or some other regularly scheduled payment plan. Many have specifically designed food products, which are purchased weekly for an additional 40 to 60 dollars.

Health clubs are a whole 'nother kettle of poached fish. Monthly membership fees and long-term contract commitments are only the tip of the aerobic iceberg.

Exercise clubs and spas *require* (*it's in the contractual fine print*) a complete new aesthetically correct wardrobe, beginning with neon-colored spandex shorts, halter top, leotard and brand name workout shoes.

I've never found just the right shade of neon-colored spandex to go with the bright red flush that comes to my face during even the mildest exertion, and I'd rather run naked through the streets than be caught in any type of leotard. Leotards look cute on six-year-olds. After that an ace bandage or a plaster cast is quite sufficient to shrink-wrap aging body parts.

But the hot topic in the lunchroom in January often revolves around who's doing what to trim down: Cost and comparison of exercise bikes, treadmills, aerobics classes, workout videos, you name it. And I was tired of having nothing to add to the conversation.

"Jan," said Anna Marie, opening one of the larger boxes, "did you order this *pillow?*"

"It's the free dividend I got for responding before January 31st."

"Start at the beginning," said Anna Marie. "This ought to be good."

"Remember a couple of Sundays ago when I spent the afternoon in meditation recharging my spiritual batteries?"

"I remember the weekend you didn't get off the couch except to use the bathroom and fix another sandwich."

"Yeah, well, *anyway*... I was watching this Infomercial, and—"

"An *infomercial?*" interrupted Anna Marie. "What happened? Couldn't you reach the remote control?"

"No— wait— this one was different."

"How so?"

"There were all these testimonials by all these average, ordinary, previously overweight individuals who've lost tons and tons of weight, trimmed down, toned up and are living happily ever after.

"Everyone was crying and carrying on and so delighted to be on camera for their 15 seconds of fame, that I got to thinking: If these people can do it, so can I."

"But what makes this program different from all the others?" asked my ever-skeptical friend.

"For one low payment I get *everything* I need: Vitamins, water filters, record book, videos, *and* the free bonus pillow."

"And what, pray tell, is this miracle regime called?"

"Sofa Snoozing to Slimness." I beamed. "First I take my multi-vitamin supplements, wash them down with only the purest carbon-filtered water, record the date and time in my personalized record book and pop the video into the VCR.

"By the time the first group of scrunchy-sock chubbettes start bumping and grinding to the strains of 'I Can't Get No Satisfaction,' I'm supposed to plump the pillow, sprawl out on the couch and enjoy the show until I fall asleep. Humming is optional."

"So how is that supposed to help you lose weight?"

"That's the beauty of it. For every hour I spend on the sofa, I am actually *exercising* my willpower not to eat—as long as I don't use the rest periods to raid the refrigerator. And although results may vary, most people are able to lose an entire afternoon or evening several times a week."

"Very interesting," mused Anna Marie. "It's a shame we didn't think of it first. So who's the celebrity brainchild reaping millions by endorsing it?"

"The same hopelessly energetic and squeaky-voiced guy who sells those comfy mattresses—you've probably heard of him—I think his name is Simmons."

"Of course." Anna Marie smiled. "But if it's all the same to you, I think I'll stick with my stepper."

"Whatever works."

CHAPTER FIVE
A Writer's Life

Welcome to the Club

Robert Michael Pyle, a local writer hailing from our own little Gray's River, was the inspirational/motivational speaker last month at the "Writers' Weekend at the Beach" workshop in Ocean Park. Bob is a hero of mine. It's a privilege to listen to him. I absorbed every word, cherishing the gems and jewels and bits of priceless information he divulged about the writing process.

But even heroes falter.

"There is no club," said Bob. *What was that? What did he say? Now wait just a darn minute! Sure there's a club,* I challenged him mutely, *and you're in it. You've arrived. You're a respected writer; a member of the inner literary circle.*

"Stephen King and Jean Auel don't think they're in the club," he went on. *Boy,* I mused, *if Bob spoke personally with Mr. King and Ms. Auel, then he's really pushing this "no club" act a bit too far. We "commoners" would never get an audience with the likes of them.*

Of course there's a club! I imagined myself shrieking. *If there's no club, what's the point? Do you think I'm writing just for personal satisfaction? We all came to this conference to learn how to join the club, and now you're insisting there's no such thing!*

Looking around for validation, I noted that the others in the group were all nodding their heads sagely and taking copious notes. I kept still. Later, in the privacy of my own home, I pondered Bob's words, even those to which I took exception.

The words came back to me again in a flash last weekend. I was in Tacoma to teach at the Pacific Northwest Writers' Conference for high school students. These teenagers gave up a Saturday to learn about writing. Most of them paid a small tuition to be there. This was the best of both possible worlds for me—teaching and writing. Perhaps *now* I would be considered a member of that elite group whose existence Bob denied. I was in my height of glory.

It was short lived.

At the end of my two-hour session on writing feature articles and personal experience columns, I opened the class up for questions.

"Are you ever going to write a *real* book?" asked the owner of first hand raised.

"Yeah," chimed in another, "my English teacher says that newspaper journalists are all frustrated novelists." In the farthest recesses of my mind the seeds of doubt were firmly planted:

"Those who can write, do. Those who fake it work for small town newspapers and teach workshops."

The drive home was a somber one. My self-esteem floundered; I searched for my bootstraps. I tried to find comfort in past achievements. After all, I've received a few awards for my columns. And I have loyal readers. Heck, I even got *paid* to teach for the PNWC. Surely now I was considered a *real* writer.

Keeping one hand on the steering wheel, I reached

for my purse and pulled out the check I'd obtained from the conference board. Yes! There it was—tangible proof that my expertise was valuable, that I was *somebody.*

I flipped on the dome light. The check was made out to me, all right. That was *my name* clearly written at the top. But wait. . .there was something missing. On the line at the bottom of the check where the signature should have been, there was no signature.

I tried not to take it personally.

By the time I turned at Johnson's Landing I had the whole odyssey in perspective. The preparation for my maiden workshop had taken weeks. I bought a new outfit for the occasion. I spent the sleepless night before in a cheesy motel. I drove 320 miles and used approximately 12 gallons of gas. I had hired someone to house sit and feed my cat. Once the check is signed and cashed I will come out just twenty dollars in the hole.

I'm ready now to concur with Bob: there is no club. But there *is* an initiation.

Scared Silly

"It was a dark and stormy night," I began.

"Now *that's* original," interrupted Anna Marie.

"It *was* a dark and stormy night," I said. "Saturday before last—remember all the thunder and lightning?"

"And I suppose this has nothing whatsoever to do with the fact that next week is Halloween?"

"Absolutely not."

"Then by all means, continue."

"It was a dark and stormy night," I began again.

"I believe we've established that."

"Look, are you going to let me tell it MY way, or are you going to keep breaking the mood, here? Mood is very important to this story."

Anna Marie pressed her lips together and pretended to zip them shut. *Not such a bad idea*, I thought. I got up from the kitchen table to fix us another cup of tea. Let her wait.

A few weeks ago I took a novel writing seminar from Enes Smith, a writer from Bend, Oregon. I enrolled in the class not because I thought there's a novel or two lurking deep within me, but because I needed a jump start, of sorts, to get me back to the keyboard in earnest. Writers feed off other writers. Creativity is contagious.

As it turned out, Enes Smith writes suspense novels. I'd never read a suspense novel. Not one. But I figured, correctly, that being well-versed in this specific genre wasn't a prerequisite to participating in the seminar.

I actually learned quite a bit. And somewhere deep within me germinated a small seed of an idea that maybe, just maybe, I DO have a novel or two lurking in there. And sometime during the 6 hours of instruction, it dawned on me that one must read in the genre in which one chooses to write.

Long before I started writing a column of my own, I was a fan of Erma Bombeck, Tom Bodett, Ruthe Stein and Dave Barry. So I figured it couldn't hurt to start doing a little research into the suspense arena—just in case.

I traded Smith one of my books for one of his. My choice was simple—I have only one book out. In return, Smith gave me his first novel: *Fatal Flowers.*

Years ago, I *enjoyed* scaring the socks off myself. As a teen, I often piled into a fire engine red '55 Buick with five other young women and headed for the Sno-King drive-in theater in Lynnwood. The driver skillfully maneuvered the tank-like vehicle between the speaker posts and we settled in to watch Vincent Price leer his way across the screen as the unstoppable "Dr. Phibes." Remembering scenes from "Jaws" and "Wait till Dark" still gives me goose bumps.

But somewhere along the trail to adulthood I gave up scary movies, opting instead for light romantic comedies and an occasional spy thriller. I haven't seen a horror flick since horror flicks became so full of horror.

Although psychology is an interest of mine, I wasn't interested in seeing "Silence of the Lambs." I mention this particular movie because when Ann Rule, who wrote the nonfiction book *Small Sacrifices*, endorsed Smith's *Fatal Flowers*, she drew a comparison to "Silence of the Lambs."

Had I seen the movie, I might have had a clue.

"Do I have to beg?" asked Anna Marie. "When are

you going to tell me what happened?"

I placed a fresh cup of tea in front of her and spoke in a whisper: "The wind howled through the trees. Lightning and thunder ripped open the sky so close together there was no time to count 'one Mississippi, two Mississippi…' The house joists creaked and groaned and strained against the gale. Tree branches assaulted the rooftop at irregular intervals.

"I lit a half dozen candles and placed them on the bed stand. My heavy-duty, high-powered, battery-operated lantern stood ready. I hunkered down under the comforter and continued reading, determined to help capture the madman dumping the remains of women near a small town on the southern Oregon coast.

"Rain beat against my window; the driveway was flooded. The tunnel near the fictional town of Newharbor had succumbed to the heavy rains as well. My vivid imagination crossed the line from reality to fantasy…"

"And then?" prompted Anna Marie.

"And then I stayed up half the night reading, and the other half I was wide awake listening to things that go bump in the night."

Anna Marie laughed. "So I guess you won't be reading any more of *those* books for awhile, huh?"

"Actually," I replied, "I'd like to do a little more research in this genre." I drained my teacup. "Besides," I continued, "what better way to spend a dark and stormy night?"

"And the Winner Is…"

Everyone gets 15 minutes of fame in his or her lifetime. But not everyone would go to the same lengths to achieve their brief notoriety.

To get my time in the limelight I drove 680 miles, shot one whole weekend, survived an armpit-puddling 86 degree eastern Washington heat wave, and spent at least a bazillion hours in the car conversing nonstop with my mother. Yes, my mother.

"Since you have to go right by my front door on your way to Wenatchee," she said in a phone call last month, "I could ride along with you."

It seemed like a good idea at the time.

I picked her up early Saturday morning. Mom was in heaven; I was a captive audience. She got out her notepad. "I've made a little list of things I need to talk to you about," she said as she flipped through page after page. "You haven't visited me in months."

"This is not a guilt trip," I told her. "This trip is for the sole purpose of tooting my own horn, basking in the sun, taking my bows in a public forum, and receiving unmitigated adulation from my journalism peers." Ah, how idealistic I was—how unprepared for reality!

Two years ago I received first place for my column in the Washington Newspaper Publisher Association's annual contest. The presentation was in Yakima that year, and I did not attend.

Last year the banquet was held in Spokane—much too far to consider. I took third.

When the WNPA notified me in August that I was again among the finalists, I discovered the awards would be given out in Wenatchee. I lived in Wenatchee for a year just after college. Wenatchee is a beautiful town, especially in the fall. A Saturday in Wenatchee was "doable."

The contest guidelines call for submissions of three representative articles, dated May 1 through April 30 of the previous year. Two of those entries must be in consecutive issues.

I keep track of the responses my writing generates. The articles I submitted received far and away the most positive reader reaction and universal identification.

"Of mice and men and practical jokes" was the story of a naked, near-sighted, semi-hysterical woman engaged in a vicious broom-battle with a rubber rat strategically placed by a prankster in her bathroom mousetrap.

The following edition contained "If it's Tuesday, it must be Belgium," a tongue-in-cheek review of the movie "Free Willy," whose PG rating apparently stood for "Poor Geography."

"Girls' Night Out" completed the package, a playful jab at restaurant dining with a contingent of picky women eaters.

There's something quite humbling about walking into the Red Lion convention rooms and rubbing shoulders with journalistic types from all over the state. Not thinking I'd know anyone there, I was pleasantly surprised to run into Marc Stiles, Elizabeth Parker and Craig Dennis, all formerly of the *Observer*. I was thankful we were competing in different divisions.

Mom and I perused the photo entries and took seats near the center of the room. From there we could clearly see the three large screens adjacent to the podium. Clusters of writers and photographers and editors and advertising representatives warmed up their noise-makers. The air was electric.

As each award was announced, slides of the winning entries came up on the screens: to the left was third, to the right was second, and first place filled the middle section. Comments from the judges were read for each first place.

For almost two hours we paid tribute to spot news, features, sports, layout and design, ads and special sections, ad infinitum. At last the category for "Best Humorous Column" was announced. My heart stood still. The emcees called out the winners for Divisions I and II, and then made some small talk. The *Chinook Observer* is in Division III.

I looked at Mom. She made a face at me. I got the giggles.

When "Through My Looking Glass" finally appeared on the screen, it was on the right hand side. Second place. "Hey!" said Mom much too loudly, "that's *my* last name up there!" And of course, good old Mom was clapping hardest of all. She told me later she'd been secretly hoping I'd get to go up and say a few words, and that I'd publicly acknowledge, once and for all, that I got my sense of humor from her.

No such luck.

At the end of the presentations I unceremoniously picked up the packet containing all ten awards garnered by the *Observer* and we headed back over the mountains. By Mom's calculations I've got roughly 13 minutes 38 seconds more "fame" coming.

We're both looking forward to next year's trip.

The Write Stuff

Creative Nonfiction. Nonfiction Storytelling. The New Journalism.

Talese, Woolfe, Capote, Mailer, Franklin, Zinsser.

Star breaks, nut grafs, echo quotes.

The words danced on the overhead projector screen. I slouched down lower in my chair. Inside the shuttered elementary classroom in Cannon Beach, it dawned on me that I was surrounded by professional journalists—people who actually make their living by writing.

Oh good Lord, I thought, just what in heaven's name have I gotten myself into now? I've finally signed up for a class I haven't a prayer of passing.

*　　*　　*

Jack Hart, writing coach for The Oregonian, brings more to the class than boyish good looks. His softly graying hair, clean-shaven face, and dimples-to-die-for, belie his expertise.

Hart knows his stuff—inside out, upside down, and backwards—and he's a damn fine teacher. When the third revision of a three-page single-spaced class syllabus arrived with still a month before the class commenced, I wondered just what kind of a man could produce such a detailed outline. "I used to be compulsive," Hart admits to the class, "I used to fold my underwear." Now his greatest obsession is with efficiency.

His files, marked Monday through Friday in clear block print, contain thick bundles of handouts. He utilizes a multi-media approach that capitalizes on different learning styles: lectures, textbooks, computer overheads, laser disks, printed samples, the blackboard. The slower writers request, and receive, copies of his lecture notes—succinct enough to be distributed without deciphering. There is never enough time to assimilate the crush of information that permeates the room.

Clak-clak-clak-clak-clak. The keyboard's staccato drumming is the only sound in the afternoon heat. There, on the overhead screen for all to see, he rearranges, modifies, deletes, expands, amazes. The speed of his editing leaves me breathless.

"Make high, sweeping circles," says Hart, motioning with his index finger in the air around his head. "Circle like a vulture about the person you're interviewing. Keep tightening that circle until you find your story. Dive in when you see the raw meat."

My volunteer interviewee, 82-year-old Margaret Sraufe, provides me with a story full of drama—complete with a tidal wave, missing son allegedly on the beach that night, and husband with a heart condition. I write my own heart out, but I think it's safe to say that my rendition of Margaret's experience will not be in contention for the Pulitzer Prize. But I think it is a very fine story, and I know I write it better because of Hart's instruction.

Feature writing is now accepted as a literature form. The New Journalism abandons the inverted pyramid style of reporting. It employs scene setting and characterization to attract readers. It's a short story in disguise, and there's really nothing "new" about it. The story entertains as well as informs, and that makes it rival the novel in terms of leisure time spent—as well as in book sales.

* * *

I took the class, offered through the Haystack extension courses sponsored by Portland State University, to expand my writing knowledge. The tuition was steep—$305. for the week. Was it worth it? Every penny. I completed the course with a great deal more than the proper pronunciation of denouement.

"Remember to begin *in media res,*" concluded Hart, "In the middle of the action. And end with a one-syllable hard consonant word that commands the reader's attention. End with a word that has punch—a crisp, sharp, vivid word—a nice strong word like 'dead'."

"Why I'm Scared at a Writers' Conference"

I can die happy now; I attended a writers' conference in Bremerton and had one of my poems shredded (*they call it critiqued*) by 45 of my peers in a workshop being led by my poetic idol.

William Stafford is unequivocally one of the greatest living poets in the Pacific Northwest. He has published nine books of poetry, won numerous literary awards, served on national poetry committees, and is, or has been, the appointed poet laureate of Oregon. The quote I used for the title of this piece was the title of the keynote speech at the conference I attended—and the speech was given by Stafford.

Maybe we're all scared at writers' conferences. There's a universality in being a little reticent to have others critique your work. In the first place, it isn't easy to spill your guts out on paper. And then to allow someone else to read your work, much less make unrestrained remarks about it, feels a lot like being the last duck in the shooting gallery.

I clearly remember the first time I asked someone to read a story I had written. I was nine. The critic was my mother. It took me 26 years to find enough courage to let her read another of my creative endeavors.

It isn't easy to take a risk, but for those of us who feel compelled to write, it's a lot harder to try to keep from writing.

As Stafford said, “I don’t know if it will mean enough to someone else, I just know that I did what I needed to do today—I wrote something.”

The peninsula is home to an abundance of closet writers. (*My own computer is actually set up in a remodeled closet, but that’s not what I mean.*) These folks are the ones who scribble a poem here, an anecdote there, and wonder if anyone else would like to hear what they have to say. They have a need to be encouraged, nurtured, and yes, critiqued.

We are fortunate on this isolated strip of sand to have the Willapa Writers’ Circle firmly established, and attending these meetings is a whole lot cheaper than attending workshops—what with the tuition, transportation, motel bills, and time involved.

This writers’ group is a reasonably safe place in which to read your work aloud. I admit it took me some time to put my writing on the line, but once I started getting feedback from other writers, I was hooked. They’re a great bunch, and they all believe in one thing, as does Stafford: “This is what I have, so this is what I give—I’m a writer.”

If you can write your name, you’re a writer. And if you can write more than your name, you can benefit by hearing what others have to say about your writing. The writer may choose to take the suggestions of the critiquers, or ignore them, but another eye or another ear often catches the little glitches we may not be able to see or hear ourselves.

Writers need other writers. Whether you write poetry, mysteries, romances, historical fiction, short stories, science fiction, fantasy, children’s books, memoirs, or dabble with some other genre, there’s a place at the table for you.

Now that I think about it, I guess I’m not really

ready to die quite yet, happy or not. After all, Stafford is just one man, with one man's opinion, and I still have a few more poems and a few more stories I need to write. And maybe, just maybe, it will mean something to someone else, and maybe it will help me learn a little more about the meaning behind one of Stafford's poems, when he says:

> "We'll dance together,
> We'll dance all the way,
> I'm not afraid any more."

Shameless Self-promotion

"The waves dashed against the rocky shore. As they receded, hazardous rocks showed on the narrow beach below…"

Okay, so it wasn't Pulitzer material, but it *was* the beginning of my very first short story. I was going to be a writer. Or maybe the President. Or perhaps an astronaut. And teaching looked like a great career too…

But deep in my heart of hearts, what I really wanted was to see my name on the cover of a book. My name, on the binding, in big black letters, right there in the bookstore window.

I was nine.

At nine, no one knows the twists and turns fate has in store. At nine, no dream is impossible. At nine, there's still plenty of time to change one's career choice a couple dozen times.

When speaking of the direction his career took while attending college, Dr. John Campiche once related, "The artists all had holes in the soles of their shoes. The doctors didn't." But Dr. John, now retired, never gave up his other dream, and his 'post-retirement' watercolors have achieved much public acclaim.

As for me, I became a teacher. No regrets; I love teaching. But for the past 32 years I never let go of my other dream either. For 32 years I've gathered 'grist for the mill.' For 32 years I've waited for this week; this is the week my 'other dream' comes true.

"Through My Looking Glass, A View from the Beach," has been published by Kaleidoscope Press in Puyallup. It is a collection of 68 columns first printed right here in the *Chinook Observer*. I've been dancing on the ceiling since February.

It was in February that Penny Lent, my editor and publisher, first offered me a contract for my book. A bona fide first-time writer's *contract*!

Last winter I taught at the "Writer's Weekend at the Beach" writing workshop in Ocean Park. There I rubbed elbows with a wide assortment of 'literary types,' from children's book authors and photo journalists to playwrights and poets and romance novelists. Ms. Lent represented publishers.

And on February 25, at exactly 4:06 p.m., she looked me straight in the eye and said, "Kaleidoscope Press would like to publish your book."

I sat in shocked silence.

"Jan?...Jan?"

"Could you hold that thought?" I asked her. "There are three or four hundred people I have to go call right this very minute." I rose to my feet, lifted my arms high enough and wide enough to embrace the entire universe and began swaying rapidly from side to side.

"Jan, what are you doing?"

"This," I beamed, "is how a fat 40 year old woman does cartwheels."

Then from February until June, all I had to do was decide *which* of almost 90 columns would be included, how to organize them, re-work and edit those which were too time-bound, figure out how to transfer the text from Macintosh to IBM, do a mock-up cover design, obtain releases from a few dozen people, have publicity photos taken, and write a mini-biography.

Since June, my major responsibility has been to chew my fingernails.

"I imagine it's a lot like being pregnant," I lamented to my friend Anna Marie. "I can't wait to see what my 'baby' looks like."

"You could spend your time figuring out how to spend your royalties," said the ever-practical Anna Marie.

She had a lot to learn—as I did. The breakdown goes something like this: the first 25 percent of the cover price goes to the printer; Pacific Pipeline gets 15 percent for promotion and distribution; the bookstores take 40 percent to cover overhead, advertising, etc.; the publisher gets 10 percent (out of which the cover artist is paid); and, if my math is accurate, that leaves a pitiful little 10 percent for the author. In my case, it translates to a smidgen under a dollar per book.

"Keep your day job," said Anna Marie.

At 1:42 p.m. on September 29, I went into labor. "The manuscript is on the way to the printer," said my publisher.

My publisher. Two of the prettiest sounding words this side of heaven. Little did she know she'd also have to serve as my Lamaze coach. "The first one's the hardest," she assured me, "but in six more weeks you'll have something to brag about."

It took a full nine months from contract to book signing, but it was well worth the wait. In the interim I've been practicing my signature.

...and how would you like *your* book signed?

The Final Word

The business portion of the weekly Willapa Writers' Circle meeting concluded with miscellaneous writing opportunities and announcements.

"Eureka!" said Birdie, "is the theme for next quarter's 'Thema' magazine. The deadline is July first."

"Eureka?" I queried, tongue-in-cheek. "Do you think very many people will have something to write about vacuum cleaners?" My attempted humor was met with a variety of rolled eyes and veiled smirks. I kept going, hoping for a bigger laugh. "My mother once received a vacuum cleaner for Mother's Day. As I recall, she wasn't as thrilled as we thought she'd be...maybe I could write a story about that." Still not much response.

"You thought vacuum cleaners," said another woman in the group, "I immediately thought of Eureka, California."

"*Eureka*!" repeated Birdie with great emphasis, gesturing to the exclamation point.

"I found it!" said Bill.

"I've got it!" said Ellen.

"I *still* don't get it!" I chimed in, finally hearing the laughter I craved. "From what language do we get 'Eureka' anyway?"

"Greek," said one.

"Latin," suggested another.

"Californian?" said a woman at the end of the table.

"No…it is Greek," concurred the original Latin proponent, consulting her pocket dictionary. "It's attributed to Archimedes on discovering a method for determining the purity of gold. It's now used to express triumph on discovery. I must have been thinking about excelsior."

"The sword?" I asked with mock innocence.

"Excalibur was King Arthur's sword!" exclaimed Birdie. "Excelsior was a mountain or something."

"I believe the Excelsior diamond is one of the largest diamonds in the world," said California woman.

"Nevertheless, " I mumbled, "I'm still pretty sure Eureka IS a brand of vacuum cleaner…"

"Oh, you…" Birdie waved her papers in my direction. "You started this on purpose, didn't you? Just so you'd have something to write about in your column."

"Well, maybe…" I smiled. "But I'm still not sure how Xavier fits into all this…"

"Any other announcements," interjected Bonnie, "before we move on to critiques this evening?"

"Killjoy," I whispered in her direction, picking up my pen and reluctantly settling down to business.

I have always loved words. Big words, little words, words with rhythm and texture and meat on their bones. Sweet words that roll like honey off the tongue; sharp words that snap and pop like a forest fire; juicy words that conspire, inspire or fuel passionate desire.

Eureka! Excelsior! Excalibur! Xavier! Viva la vocabulary!

"The difference between the right word and the almost right word," said American humorist Mark Twain, "is the difference between lightning and the lightning bug."

Mark Twain, born Samuel Clemens, knew well the merit of mincing words. His pseudonym was derived from terminology used by Mississippi river boatmen as they monitored the depths of the water beneath the hull. "Mmm—aark Twaa—ain," they called out, "Mark Twain." Two fathoms deep—safe water.

Not all writers need to be that deep. All they need is a genuine desire to share the wealth of words they treasure, knowing that well-chosen alliteration, picturesque prose, or a craftily constructed simile can ignite the imagination of even the most passive reader.

And when a reader connects with a writer who fires his or her imagination, it's a match made in heaven.

Looking back over the last few lines, a subtle extended metaphor jumps right off the page. "Ignite... fire... match." Going back a few more paragraphs I can add "forest fires, lightning and fuel."

Burning hot within me (okay, I admit I'm pushing the metaphor here) is the dream of finding the ever-illusive spark of linguistic genius to make myself immortal.

For, if the truth be told, isn't that one reason why writers write? To insure that a part of them will go on living long after the dust has settled in their wake? (*Or should that be "at their wake?" Whatever...*)

All I can say for certain is that the rush of unmitigated joy whenever I see my byline makes wrestling with the keyboard well worth the effort. I write because I cannot not write. We writer-types have things to say, things to share—like the value of a whimsical word or creative twist of phrase.

George Lucas, the brainchild behind the "Star Wars" phenomenon, knows the value of such words—especially at the box office. Not only did he make "Wookie" a household name, but he encouraged fledgling writers everywhere with his inspirational exhortation, "Metaphors be with you!"

Eureka! Pure gold!

CHAPTER SIX
Friends and Family

Hostage Situation

I love my mother. Really, I do. But if Mom had died under mysterious circumstances during the winter of December 97's snowstorm, not a jury in the land would convict me.

Not a jury of my peers.

What began as a pleasant two-day excursion northward for a "family dinner" quickly turned into a week-long ordeal making the trials and tribulations of the Donner Party look like a cake walk.

I left on Tuesday, Christmas eve. "The five day forecast calls for highs in the upper 40s and lower 50s with a slight chance of precipitation toward the end of the week," proclaimed the radio weather person.

Great, I thought. I can come home late Thursday or early Friday and not have to worry about ice on the roads.

By Thursday afternoon, ice on the roads was the least of my worries.

I've lived in western Washington my entire life. I've seen snow before. And freezing rain. And floods. But what I saw in the week between Christmas and New Year's was a sight heretofore not imagined.

Fast and furious, the furry flakes quickly made driving anywhere out of the question. By Friday morning, a full 16 inches of snow turned my car into a giant sloping igloo. I looked at Mom. She looked at me. “I guess I’m going to be here awhile,” I said, and poured a little Bailey’s Irish Cream into my coffee.

On Saturday morning another seven or eight inches of the white stuff obliterated the trail to the mailbox. Freezing rain was predicted. I sat transfixed before the television, which now aired only news and weather.

The rain started late Saturday evening. *Melt*, I prayed. But it didn’t melt. The combined weight of snow and frozen water became the hot news topic. Store roofs succumbed to the pressure. Marinas caved in on hundreds of yachts. A quarter million people in the Puget Sound region were without electricity as falling trees wiped out power lines.

“We could be worse off,” I told Mother Sunday morning. “We have heat and lights and plenty of food left from Thursday’s gathering.”

And then the carport collapsed.

Kaboom! In the space of a single heartbeat, twisted metal and a mountain of snow slammed into the side of the mobile home. Luckily, no windows were broken, but the position of the wreckage effectively trapped us inside. Although I had cleared snow away from the back door the day before, drifts during the night blocked the alternate exit.

I looked at Mom. She looked at me. I poured a little more Bailey’s into my coffee.

“I don’t mean to be critical,” she said a short time later, “but isn’t that the same outfit you wore yesterday?”

I pulled my bathrobe snugly about me and replied, “Do you see any real point in my getting dressed?”

I set the coffee cup on top of the television and

flipped through the channels. Mom picked up my mug and wiped for rings beneath it.

I opened several containers of holiday goodies and set a hearty meal of fudge and cookies and nut clusters on a plate in front of the TV. Before I could return to the kitchen, Mom put the lids back on the canisters and the milk back in the fridge.

"How big is this mobile home?" I asked her.

"Fourteen by 70, but that includes the hitch."

"So we're talking approximately 980 square feet of living space, right?"

"More like 900," said Mom. "Not counting the walls, the cupboards, the counters, the appliances, the furniture…"

I looked at Mom. She looked at me. "Where's this water coming from?" she asked, running a sponge across the counter where I had assembled my breakfast.

Traced to its source, the water was coming from damage done to the roof edge when the carport gave way. Two streamlets ran down the wallpaper inside the cupboard from the ceiling to the paper towel dispenser below where accumulating water threatened to seep inside an electrical outlet.

"Got any duct tape?" I asked, perching precariously on the counter top. "Got any plastic food wrap?"

Mom handed both items up to me and I constructed a makeshift drainpipe, funneling the water from the leak directly into the sink.

"How'd you figure that out?" asked Mom.

"I watch McGyver."

My window of opportunity came the next day. If I didn't leave then, who knew how long the roads might be flooded…

Wading through knee-deep slush between the back entrance and the street, my brother helped me to my car.

"How'd it feel being sequestered with Mom for a week?" he asked. "I'm surprised you two didn't kill each other."

I smiled as I hugged him good-bye. "Not guilty," I replied.

The Nicest Thing About Mom

Mom turns 29 on the 29th. She's done that every year since I can remember. That's okay by me; I figure we should all pick out a year we really like and stay there. Mom will always be 29, bless her heart.

Anyway, Mom completed another circuit around the sun today, and I've been doing some thinking about that.

I've thought about the endless trips Mom made up and down the stairs with loads upon loads of laundry during my youth. I've thought about the shoes lined up on the kitchen counter Sunday mornings waiting to be polished before church. I've thought about the sandwiches and homemade cookies Mom packed into lunch boxes as the four of us kids progressed through school. I've thought about the countless hours spent sitting at the kitchen table as she helped us with homework and drilled us on our spelling lists.

I bet she thinks I've forgotten when she covered for me as I occasionally tiptoed in a little after curfew, or the 20-dollar bills she slipped me during my college years. She might even think I'm not appreciative of the hours she spent at the ironing board on my behalf, or the times she was called in for a conference with the principal because my school behavior was less than perfect.

She's wrong. I do remember, and I do appreciate every single thing she's ever done for me.

Funny thing about mothers and daughters. Most times we just naturally figure it goes without saying that we care about each other. But every so often my conscience reminds me that it's not wise to assume too much. For the record, I'm going public: I love my mother.

I got my sense of humor from Mom's side of the family. During the past four years I've occasionally written familial anecdotes in this column to illustrate what I hoped was an amusing point. That's why it blew me away when Mom took me to task a few months ago.

"When are you going to write something nice about your mother?" she queried.

"Huh?" (*My usual witty repartee failed me.*)

"Anybody reading your column would think your mother is a terrible person. I imagine that if I visited you in Long Beach people would point and stare."

"You're imagining, all right."

"Have you considered that what you put in writing is a legacy for my grandchildren? Why do you always portray me in such a derogatory way?"

Now I was really in the dark. In my mind, any references to my mother painted only a positive, enlightening, encouraging, sometimes silly, but always loving portrait. (*Okay, okay, maybe once or twice I've taken a snipe-shot, but I wasn't aiming at anyone except perhaps the Ozzie and Harriet stereotype.*)

When I've written about 'Mom,' I was often writing about 'Everymom'—the woman we all had, could have had, might have had or wished we had, during our formative years. My columns are for entertainment, not strict historical documentation. I tried to explain that to her, but I guess I botched it.

"You used 'Mom' with a capital 'M'," she continued. "That could only mean me." She sighed. "I swear, Janet

Marie, there are times when I wish I could have your poetic license revoked."

Janet Marie? Whenever she uses my given first and middle names I know she's serious. I was walking a tightrope here. Even though I knew in my heart that I had never written anything intentionally embarrassing, humiliating or out of line, I figured an apology couldn't hurt.

"I love you, Mom."

"I know. That's why I haven't written a letter to your editor telling my side of some of your stories. I love you too."

The phone line between us became uncharacteristically quiet.

"So when are you going to write something nice about your mother?" she asked again.

"Your birthday's coming up," I told her. "We'll see…"

So to celebrate Mom's birthday, her 29th birthday, if she really wants to insist that I stick to writing only the absolute, unadorned and/or unembellished truth, then I suppose I'll have to be honest about her age as well. Truth is…truth is, Mom's really a couple years older than 29.

But that's beside the point. The point of this column was to say something especially nice about my mother. And the nicest thing about her, the very nicest thing, is that Mom has always lovingly put up with me.

Thanks, Mom, and Happy Birthday.

Caustic, Cosmic and Pushy
PART I

"I think we should go," said Pushy.

Cosmic looked doubtful. "I'll take it under consideration."

And I, being Caustic, replied, "Oh, sure…and just how much will *this* little adventure cost me?"

"The bus is free," said Pushy.

"The price certainly sounds right," said Cosmic.

"What's the catch?" I asked.

"Well," hedged Pushy, "the bus leaves Warrenton at 8 a.m. and returns around 6 p.m. the same day."

Cosmic quickly counted on her fingers. "That's only four hours in the casino."

I rolled my eyes. "I don't know about you guys, but I can lose plenty of money in four hours."

"Or *win* plenty of money…" mused Cosmic.

"Look," said Pushy, "by some twist of fate, we can all clear our schedules for the next bus run. It'll be fun—the three of us have never taken a road trip together."

Cosmic grinned. "Then," she said, winking in my direction, "that certainly settles it…it was meant to be."

"I'll make the reservations," said Pushy.

"And I'll take out a bank loan," I sighed.

The morning of our departure the bus was running a half hour late. "Sorry about the delay," said the driver. "Since Highway 101 is still closed south of Cannon Beach we have to take 53 into Wheeler."

"Highway 53?" I asked. "Along the Miami? You've got to be kidding. That detour makes the road around Willapa Bay look straight."

"Are you going or not?" asked Pushy. "If you're going with us, I suggest you quit jawing and get on board."

Pushy clambered up the steps and took a seat right up front—I suspected she wanted to keep one eye on the driver and one eye on the road. Cosmic sat right behind her. I, of course, located myself strategically between the bathroom and the emergency exit.

The trip south, albeit slow and curvaceous, passed uneventfully. Arriving at Chinook Winds in Lincoln City, I wondered if perhaps the casino had been misnamed. I suspected Chinook WINS might be a more appropriate moniker.

A friendly casino worker met us at the door and passed out gift packs of playing cards and discount coupons. "Be sure to wear your identifying fish tag," she said. "Then we'll know you came here with a tour."

I looked skeptically at the fuzzy green pom-pom fish. "Is this supposed to be a Chinook salmon?" I asked.

"I don't think so," said Pushy, "it's too round."

Cosmic agreed. "It has a round mouth, too. It looks more like a sucker to me."

"In that case," I replied, "I think I'll wear it on my forehead."

It's amazing how quickly time passes when you're busy shoving money into a bottomless pit. All too soon, our four-hour odyssey was over.

Pushy, no longer a casino virgin, had been sacrificed to the glorious gods of the plastic push-button bandits. Although she began with the usual amount of beginner's luck, it had been short-lived. Not only did her hot gambling hand turn cold, but we now refer to her as Madam Frigidaire.

Cosmic, true to form, became instantly engulfed in exactly the right-colored aura (*I think they were red, white and blue sevens*), and emerged the 'big winner' of our group.

And I, being ever-so-slightly obsessive/compulsive, had positioned myself for the final three hours at a single slot machine, sure it would only be a matter of a few more minutes before it paid off big.

As the bus began loading for the return trip, I speedily cashed in my voucher and bolted for the door. Rumor has it that I knocked four people down while running for the motor coach. It wasn't so much a matter of my wanting to hurry home as it was the terror of possibly seeing someone else strike it rich on the very machine I'd been playing all afternoon.

"So how'd you do?" asked Pushy as I settled back into my seat.

"Absolutely fantastic," I told her.

Cosmic turned around to meet my gaze. "Oh, really?"

"You bet," I smiled. "All I've consumed today is five crackers and six diet Pepsis. I didn't even *think* about eating while I was gambling. I could make a fortune with this. I think I'll call it the 'Casino Diet.' It's a shoo-in for the Diet-of-the-Month club. Just you wait—I'm gonna be rich."

"So you didn't win any money today?" asked Cosmic.

"Not a cent." I shook my head. "But I sure had fun."

Caustic, Cosmic and Pushy
PART II

When we last left our three friends—Caustic, Cosmic and Pushy—they had just returned to Warrenton, virtually unscathed, from their grueling all-day bus ride to the casino in Lincoln City.

But the trip wasn't over yet.

"Since I'm the *Big Winner*," said a most magnanimous Cosmic, "it seems only fair that I buy dinner."

"I wouldn't want you to spend it all in one place," I said hesitantly.

Pushy elbowed me. "It sounds great. Where'll we eat?"

"Let's have Chinese," said Cosmic, as we walked to my car.

"There's got to be a catch," I muttered. "There's *always* a catch."

"*Of course* there's a catch," said Cosmic, "but I'll tell you what it is *after* we get to the restaurant."

The waitperson seated us and distributed menus. Cosmic immediately requested some barbecued pork. "And we'll be eating with chopsticks," she said with quiet authority.

"Chopsticks?!" Pushy and I said in unison.

"That's the catch," said Cosmic. She smiled serenely, rested her elbows on the edge of the table and pressed the tips of her fingers together. "I want you to appreciate the whole experience of Chinese cuisine."

"Not me," said Pushy. "If I try eating with chopsticks I'll be wearing most of my dinner home on my shirt front."

The waitperson brought the appetizer and asked if we were ready to order.

"If you're serious about this," I whispered to Cosmic, "then I'm skipping the soup course."

As she delivered a fresh pot of tea, our server placed a set of paper-wrapped chopsticks beside each teacup. Cosmic, with the speed of light, began collecting the utensils from each place.

Realizing she was about to attack a plate of vegetables, rice and spareribs armed only with two thin sticks of wood, Pushy hastily grabbed her spoon. She waved it in the air. "I'm hanging on to this just in case!" she exclaimed, and stuck it triumphantly into her jacket pocket—safely out of Cosmic's reach.

"Waitress!" exclaimed an overly-dramatic Cosmic, "this woman is stealing the silver!"

"Don't worry," I said to her, "I'm sure they can put it on the bill—you DID say you were buying, didn't you?"

"Dinner," said Cosmic, feigning dignity usually reserved for British royalty, "does not include individual place settings."

Amazingly, Cosmic and I managed to eat our meals by carefully maneuvering our chopsticks. Pushy, true to her prediction, dropped a few noodles onto her clothing. "Snacks for later," she said good-naturedly.

"Why don't you use your spoon?" asked Cosmic.

"A spoon wouldn't help much on these noodles," said Pushy with a small, pitiful sigh.

Cosmic relented and handed over a fork.

At the meal's conclusion, I was erroneously given the wrong fortune cookie—or so I tried to convince the other two.

"Come on, guys," I said, "it's obvious I should have gotten Pushy's fortune promising creativity and talent. Or even Cosmic's cookie complimenting my class and style."

Cosmic choked. Pushy laughed.

"You had first choice on the cookies," said Pushy.

"I didn't want to be RUDE—I just took the cookie closest to me. The plate must have been turned as it was set on the table."

"In the future," said Cosmic, "you'll have to remember that the closest cookie isn't necessarily the best one for you."

How true! I thought. *How true!*

We were half way across the Megler/Astoria bridge before Pushy discovered her latent tendencies toward kleptomania. "Oh my God!" she exclaimed. "Oh my God!"

"What's the matter?" asked Cosmic as I applied heavy pressure to the brake pedal.

"We have to go back!" wailed a semi-hysterical Pushy.

"Did you forget something?" asked Cosmic. "Do you have your pocketbook?"

"The spoon!" exclaimed Pushy. "I've still got the spoon!"

We laughed till it hurt, then Cosmic turned around and addressed our sticky-fingered friend, "at least now you're not going home from our casino adventure empty-handed."

"Oh yes I am," said Pushy, wiping tears of mirth from her eyes. "While you two were busy laughing, I wiped my fingerprints off the spoon and stuck it inside Caustic's purse!"

In reality, none of us went home empty-handed. We had had a day full of laughter, friendship and memories. (*Of course, it's always possible the other two women will remember the day somewhat differently, but I'm fairly certain we'll still be speaking after they read my version of it...*)

Good friends and good times—it doesn't get any better than this.

I returned the spoon the very next night.

Sweet Baby Love

At 41 years old I finally attended my first baby shower. Not that I haven't been *invited* to a baby shower before, but until now I've avoided them for the simple reason that I thought they might be somehow contagious. Kind of like catching the bridal bouquet.

But at 41 I figure I'm relatively safe; no storks loom on the horizon. Nevertheless, it took my friend Googie, party-giver extraordinaire and mother of the expectant, some pretty fancy talking to convince me to show up.

"We're having a garden party, a luncheon," said Googie, handing me the invitation.

"I'll send a nice present along with my regrets," I told her.

"This baby shower won't be like any others," she promised.

"How would I know? I have no basis for comparison."

"Costumes optional," she said.

"Costumes?" At least she'd gotten my attention.

"Some of us are dressing up as our favorite kid," she explained. "Pippi Longstockings, Little Orphan Annie, Raggity Ann—you get the idea."

"Has anyone chosen to come as Wednesday Addams?" I asked, tongue-in-cheek. "I can see me now—pigtails, dour expression, dressed totally in black and carrying a headless doll."

Googie ignored me and threw her trump card. "There'll be men at the shower," she said. "Single men."

Okay, so maybe it *was* time I broadened my horizon…

I arrived at one o'clock on a glorious Saturday afternoon. The sun shone warmly; a gentle breeze turned the garden into a softly swaying pastel rainbow.

The food was to die for. We lunched on baked salmon, mussels on the half-shell, pea salad, stuffed mushrooms, a killer fruit plate, and a great spinach dip with chips. A variety of flowers floated in the punchbowl.

Along with the foods I easily recognized were foreign foods: shish kebab, gazpacho and vichyssoise, hailing respectively from Turkey, Spain and France. Not one to miss an educational opportunity, I learned that the spicy red/orange cold soup was gazpacho, and the white cold soup was vichyssoise. I became partial to vichyssoise.

So far this baby shower thing wasn't such a bad idea.

After the luncheon it was time for the mother-to-be to open her gifts. Ever the organizer, I thought maybe someone should coordinate the "oohs" and the "aahs" as each present was unwrapped. No luck. Some guys (and I don't use the word "guys" here accidentally) are just hopelessly incorrigible, bless their hearts.

As the growing pile of baby-loot was tallied and duly appreciated, most of us moved our chairs into the shadier areas of the garden. Several people sprawled out on the cool grass. One fine fellow took a short nap.

But for me, the best was yet to come, and no, I'm not referring to the scrumptious chocolate mousse layer cake.

"In our family we have kind of a tradition," Googie's daughter began. "And continuing that tradition, I have chosen two people to ask to be my child's fairy godparents."

Fairy Godparents? I leaned over to ask Googie to clarify, but the mom-in-waiting supplied the missing details.

"A fairy godparent is someone who can bring magic, wonder and education into my child's life. Give a different perspective. Someone who can share unusual experiences, change pumpkins into carriages, teach new games, be there to talk with and to encourage him or her.

"Jan," she continued, "would you be my child's fairy godmother?"

I looked quickly to the right and then to the left. Apparently I was the only 'Jan' in the group.

"*Me*?" I asked, still unsure I had heard correctly. "You want *me* to be the fairy godmother?"

"She did not come to this decision lightly," said Googie.

A large lump of tangible emotion lodged itself in my throat. I was afraid I couldn't speak. All eyes turned my way. After what seemed like a decade, I finally managed to nod and choked out, "I would be honored."

"Congratulations," said several party-goers.

"I suppose I *am* qualified," I smiled. "I already have a magic wand." Immediately I began planning how best to spoil this very special child. I'm eagerly looking forward to his/her arrival.

In a day filled with firsts, I attended a baby shower, ate gazpacho, and became a fairy godmother. Googie, anticipating her first grandchild, says there will be lots and lots of other firsts for both of us in the baby department. She swears she's even going to trap me into changing my first diaper.

But I wouldn't bet on it.

"It's a Boy!"

Reports of an over-anxious, hypertensive, semi-hysterical woman requiring sedation after accidently beaning someone with a rainbow-colored wand in the maternity waiting room of Columbia Memorial hospital last week have been grossly exaggerated.

Well, mostly.

It's true that I might have been a teensy-weensy bit zealous. And it's true that I was enthusiastically waving my magic wand and occasionally leading cheers during the seemingly endless days and hours we waited for the newborn's arrival. But the rumor that someone got beaned is absolutely ridiculous.

Beginning with my attendance at Lavida's baby shower, I was transformed into some type of strange machismo-maternalistic whirlwind. (*The second definition of machismo is "an exhilarating sense of power or strength."*) From the moment she appointed me 'Fairy Godmother' I vowed to be the best one that ever lived.

I took an active part in choosing a name for the baby. None of the 134 names I came up with were ultimately chosen, but at least I tried. I called several times each day to see how 'we' were doing. I asked repeatedly if the mommy-in-waiting was ready to take a long, bumpy car ride in the hopes of speeding things up a little.

My hospital bag had been packed for a month. It contained a camera, two rolls of film, a half-dozen crossword puzzle books, an equal number of sharpened pencils, a cribbage board, four decks of cards, peanuts for protein, hard candy for a quick energy boost, an extra notebook, and, of course, my magic wand.

By most calculations, the baby was due on or about Friday the 15th. Friends and relatives picked numbers to see who could hit the actual birth date.

"She's not going to have it tonight," the expectant first-time grandmother told me on Saturday. "I haven't got any make-up on. She's my daughter, she wouldn't do that to me."

"Humor me," I told Lavida on Sunday, "try jumping up and down while repeating 'I'm tired of being pregnant, I'm tired of being pregnant, I'm tired of being pregnant.'"

On Monday morning Lavida went in for a routine check-up. Her doctor put her on an intravenous 'drip' that was supposed to induce labor. I called her room Monday afternoon. 'The Man from Lamaze' answered the phone.

"How's it going, Coach?" I asked.

"Same old, same old," he replied. "We're watching soap operas."

Early Monday evening the doctor turned off the drip. "We'll try again tomorrow," she said. Easy for her to say. She was probably the only one in the entourage with any fingernails left.

At noon Tuesday Lavida got dressed and prepared to be discharged from the hospital. She was still pregnant. "I guess it just isn't time yet," she told her Lamaze coach, and sat down to wait for her ride home.

At this precise moment, her water broke.

Yet it was another full day before we got to greet the bouncing baby boy. I think he purposefully waited to be born on the 20th—the day his grandmother picked in the

Baby Lottery.

He was just about an hour and a half old when it was my turn to hold him. Eight pounds two ounces of flailing arms and legs capped by a halo of fuzzy black hair. Words failed me. I'd had months to prepare just the right speech for this auspicious occasion, and here I was—totally dumbfounded. In a soft panic, I began reciting the multiplication tables to him. His grandmother looked at me in shocked disbelief.

"It's never too early," I said without apology.

"Aren't you the one who made fun of me for reading him classic literature while he was still in the womb?"

I humbly relinquished the child to her, picked up my magic wand, and began blessing everyone connected with this precious infant.

"Is it okay if I write about his birth in my column?" I asked Lavida. "A lot of people have been asking me if I'm a Fairy Godmother yet, but I don't want to write anything that would violate your privacy."

"You caught me at a good time," she answered. "I'm so jazzed about having him that I don't care what you write. He's so sweet, so perfect, so wonderful that I want to share the news with everyone."

So now it's official; I'm a bona fide F.G.M. And not that he'll be spoiled or anything, but I'm already saving up for a trip to Disneyland.

We're going to have a great time.

The ACME Glitter Sifter

"It's good to see you," said Donna, welcoming me with a hearty hug.

"Are you busy?" I asked, mindful that Steve and I had not called before stopping by.

"I'm making a birthday card for Keith. His birthday was last week, so it's already late, and I'm supposed to be working on my taxes, but—"

"Then we're not interrupting anything," I interjected. "It's obviously an A.B.T.A."

"An A.B.T.A.?"

"An Anything But Taxes Afternoon. I recognize the symptoms. You wouldn't believe how often I have an A.B.W.N.—Anything But Write Night. You should hear some of MY excuses..."

I accepted the cream soda Donna offered and pulled a chair up to the kitchen table where she was working.

"What's all this?" asked Steve, referring to the assortment of seemingly unrelated materials spread before her.

"Well," began Donna, "I wanted Keith's card to be really special. First I wrote a birthday poem for the inside of the card about watching Hale-Bopp with him, and then I painted the blue-tailed comet on the front of it."

"That explains the paper, pens and watercolors," said Steve. "But where do the hammer, cutting board and child's bracelet come in?"

"I wanted to add some glitter to the comet's tail to make it all sparkly."

"So you're pulverizing a kid's rhinestone bracelet to make glitter?"

"It's not working very well," admitted Donna.

"Why can't you just go to the store for some?"

"I only need a small amount. I asked all my neighbors if they had any…"

I pictured Donna canvassing the neighborhood with a measuring cup of some sort requesting a pinch of glitter to finish her project.

"You *really* don't want to do your taxes today, do you?" I asked.

She laughed good-naturedly. "Am I that transparent?"

"Never fear." I smiled. "This is right up my alley." I pretended to roll up my sleeves. "Got any tinsel?"

"Tinsel? No, I don't think so."

"Then I'll need a small piece of aluminum foil," I continued, "and a pair of scissors."

Donna looked skeptical.

"Don't forget," said Steve, "Jan teaches fourth grade. She can do anything…"

I kept my hands busy flaking foil into comet-sparkle while Donna and Steve and I spent a pleasant afternoon conversing.

It's funny how when friends get together, even after an extended absence of a year or two, it only takes a few minutes for the comfortable camaraderie to slide right back into place. *As familiar as a favorite pair of shoes*, I thought, *that just haven't been worn in a while.*

Our topics moved easily from comet watching to cross-country skiing, restaurants to relationships, animal welfare to memorable movies.

And we laughed a lot.

As the tiny bits of aluminum piled up on the paper towel before me, I told glittering tales of primary classrooms inundated with fairy dust. "At school the children shake glitter out of old cookie sprinkle bottles. *theoretically*, the shakers monitor portion control.

"And speaking of portion control," I continued, "I've got a small problem. These flakes are in a wide variety of sizes." I frowned in concentration. "Donna, do you happen to have a strainer?"

"Sure thing." She jumped up and reached into a drawer behind Steve.

"If she comes up with an ACME glitter sifter…" he began.

I took the strainer and carefully sifted the foil onto another paper towel. Only the finest pieces fell through. Delighted, Donna got out the rubber cement to put the finishing touches on her creation.

"That worked great," said Steve. "Now you have A and B grade glitter. And if Jan ever decides it's time to make a career change she can list this on her resumé among her many skills."

I made a face at him. "At least you could have the decency to be appropriately impressed. I didn't hear YOU coming up with any viable suggestions."

"Good job," he said, patting my shoulder. "McGyver would be proud."

Donna held up the completed card. "There," she said. "Doesn't that add something special to it? And it's all handmade—even the glitter."

Steve and I admired her handiwork and readily agreed. Then Steve stood up to signal our imminent departure.

The editor in me knew the phrase on the tip of my

tongue was an old, worn-out cliché, but it came out of my mouth anyway. "All that glitters is not gold..." I began.

"But friendships are," said Steve, completing both the thought I was attempting to express as well as our visit.

The sparkle in three pairs of eyes confirmed it.

CHAPTER SEVEN
School Daze

For Whom the Bell Tolls

At the ringing of the bell this morning, the Peninsula's 1200 school-aged children, like Pavlov's salivating dogs, rushed eagerly back into the classrooms, hungry to further their education.

In my dreams.

In reality, who is ever really ready to kiss summer goodbye, break out the fall sweaters, put on thinking caps, and seriously crack the books? Certainly not I, and I'm the teacher.

I'm one of the 75 certificated professionals (*and let's not forget the additional 72 support staff employed by the district*), whom the parents of the Peninsula entrust their treasures to. Yep, for the next nine and a half months, I have the awesome responsibility of warping and twisting a new crop of young, impressionable senses of humor.

For 34 consecutive Septembers I've been responding to the back-to-school bell in some capacity. I enjoy being on either side of the big desk; I frequently take classes so that I may stay ahead of my students. Teaching is what I know I was born to do, and not for a single heartbeat have I regretted my decision.

But last spring I did a little career evaluation, and made a small adjustment to my professional goals. I'm moving from the fourth grade, a grade which I loved every minute of, to a grade level with an unfamiliar curriculum, different scheduling concerns, higher expectations, new colleagues to work with, and a child's developmental stage that promises never a calm moment. I imagine I'm in for some sort of an awakening.

Am I nuts to leave behind the comfort of a job I could do standing on my head for the insecurity of the unknown, just because something deep inside me craves new challenges? (*That's a rhetorical question.)*

Today I face my new challenges—25 of them. I've been re-assigned to 6th grade this year. Sixth grade. Rumor has it that this is the age at which terrorist groups begin recruiting; the age when hormones grow legs and roam the halls; the onset of puberty.

Initially, when I decided to make the leap last spring, I was merely making a conscious effort to follow my training. I wanted to teach language arts (reading, writing, spelling, grammar, etc.), which was my college major and the focus of my master's degree, in a middle school setting. Only we don't have a middle school. Yet.

What we do have is a ballooning school-age population and a lack of classroom space. Every nook, cranny, hallway, cupboard and closet is being used in each of the district's schools.

In 1977, when I arrived in my first Peninsula classroom, we had only two or three classes per grade level. Today no grade has less than four sections, and most of the K-6 grades have five. All this growth, and we're still in the same four buildings.

This unconscionable warehousing could have a serious dampening effect on the morale of the staff. But it doesn't. We give each day 110%, even within these less than favorable space limitations. Your Peninsula school personnel come from the same hearty stock as the educators for generations before them.

I vividly remember Mrs. Maki, my own elementary principal. Mrs. Maki and I spent a lot of quality time together back then. She often took a deep breath, raised her eyebrows, and proclaimed as she exhaled, "This, too, shall pass." It was always a great relief to hear those words. Taking her literally, I figured at least I wasn't going to be retained in the 4th grade the following year.

But now it's with some trepidation that I leave 4th grade behind, maybe for good this time. My ultimate goal is still to teach in a middle school on the Peninsula. Is this also in my dreams? Perhaps. However this dream has a pretty good chance of materializing.

There's going to be a building bond on the ballot in November, and your vote can help make Mrs. Maki's words ring true once again—just like the bell that rang this morning.

"This is Only a Test..."

The California Test of Basic Skills (CTBS), or a similar test, will be administered next week in classrooms all across the state of Washington. A standardized test of achievement is required by the state each fall for grades 4, 8, and 11. In the Ocean Beach School District, students in grades 2 through 11 will undergo the week-long ordeal. Next spring, the 2nd through 6th graders will have to take the tests all over again. Just thinking about it makes me sick.

I deplore the way these test results are often misconstrued by some supposedly well-educated people. We are not living in Garrison Keillor's Lake Wobegon; everyone is not above average.

Nothing angers me more than seeing one district's test scores compared to another like it was some sort of sporting event. We all know statistics can lie, and at the very least, they are often a gross misrepresentation of what is really going on in the classroom.

There are 296 public school districts in our state. At each grade level the children's test scores are placed on a bell-shaped curve. Half the children will score above the median, and half will be below. There is absolutely nothing wrong with being at the 50th "percentile." If a number of districts "improve" their scores, the median moves upward proportionately. There will still be half above, and half below, the median.

Imagine 30 students taking a test of 100 math

questions. Ten of those students get 95 correct, while 10 students get 90, and the final 10 students get 85 problems right. On a standardized test, that would mean that the students getting 85% of the problems correct would be *below average.*

Far too much emphasis is placed on test scores. Too much academic time and energy is spent preparing for, and giving, these standardized tests. Last year our district spent over $3,200 on testing that is not required by the state.

These tests have only two justifiable reasons for existence. The first is to identify weaknesses in a district's curriculum so that any obvious deficiencies can be corrected. The second is to have a reference point for a child's personal development. If a child scores at the 45th percentile *every year*, then that child is having steady academic progress—there is no cause for alarm. If, however, a child has been maintaining the 45th percentile and suddenly dips to the 35th, then further assessment and possibly remediation is in order.

I have heard ungodly tales of the way these test scores are being used in some districts. Tales of evaluating teachers and administrators by the students' alleged "growth" between the fall and spring testing. We all know what a misuse of that magnitude would foster. If my continuing employment was determined by how many percentage points my children improved by, then it would be mighty tempting to teach them the test questions, and answers, during the course of the year. But what good would that do the child?

A lot of kids get stressed out over these tests. But the test is a one-time shot. Let's keep it in perspective. All it tells us is what the child was able to do at that particular time, on that particular day.

The students are not supposed to get all the answers

right. The tests provide a wide scope of skills in each subject area. After 17 years of teaching, I already know that fourth graders will score poorly on commas, quotation marks, and long division. I know this because an average 9 year old is simply not mentally ready for some of the concepts presented on the test.

It's time to put a stop to some of the popular testing misconceptions. View these tests for what they are—just one indicator of continued progress. To help your child provide an accurate measure of his or her ability on any test, follow these three simple suggestions:

--Make sure he/she gets a good night's sleep.

--A good breakfast gives the child energy; it's hard to concentrate with an empty stomach.

--Attendance is essential. Schedule dentist and doctor appointments on some other week. "Make-up tests" separate the child from the regular classroom environment, and do not always give an accurate assessment.

Above all, assure your child that the only person who fails is the one who fails to try. As teachers, all we ask is that a child do his or her best.

Surf City, U.S.A.

Teacher Inservice Day gives educators an opportunity to attend classes around the state to expand knowledge and help keep instruction up-to-date. So while some may erroneously think we teachers have a "day off," many of us actually put in 10 to 12 hours, due to the travel time it takes to reach these classes.

My Inservice Day began at exactly 4:23 a.m. That's when I got up to check the oil in my car. The oil was still there, registering right where it should on the dipstick. But for nearly an hour I'd been tossing and turning, worried that some mechanical failure would prevent my group of Ocean Beach teachers from arriving at our destination.

Our destination this day was the Educational Service District technology lab in Vancouver. Our mission was to take the first tentative baby steps along the information superhighway.

By 6 a.m. I collected my third passenger and headed over the Megler-Astoria bridge. Dawn was dawning, the soft October sun gently lifting the dewy fog from the Columbia River, and I thought once again how lucky I am to be living in God's country.

Inspired, I began to sing. *"Over the river, and through the woods, to surf the internet. We don't have a clue, what we are to do, just hope we don't get wet!"*

The groans from the backseat cut my song short. My solo was replaced by non-stop chit-chat the rest of the trip, punctuated by intermittent questions:

"Do we get to stop for coffee pretty soon?"

"Did you get *really specific* directions to this place we're going?"

"Do we get to stop for coffee pretty soon?"

"Did you bring the map with you?"

"Do we get to stop for coffee pretty soon?

"When's the next rest stop?"

We arrived at 8:20 a.m. bright-eyed, bushy-tailed, and chock-full of caffeine, to spend the day at our respective computer terminals, learning to surf the 'net, as it's called, and send and receive e-mail.

E-mail. Electronic mail. Sending messages without benefit of paper, pencil, stamp, or a six-day turn-around response time. It took me about a heartbeat to grasp the value of such a process. Eagerly, I dashed off a memo to the woman sitting behind me. "Where shall we go for lunch?"

Our noon chatter was full of the jargon. To the casual observer we might have passed for seasoned computer hackers. Well, maybe.

A little knowledge is a dangerous thing, and the afternoon session took a dip into the Twilight Zone. Messages were flying so fast and furious that it was easy to lose track of who was sending what to whom. Soon we were forwarding messages written by other class members with an "Amen" attached instead of writing a complete reply.

"Help!" said the woman next to me, "I'm caught in the Internet Web and I can't get out!"

The instructor showed her how to 'mail' information to herself and then print out the material for use in her classroom back home.

Meanwhile, I was trying to decipher a message from someone code-named "Sexy Body" who thought I had a nice smile, wondered if I really liked football, and asked if I had ever seen the Bears play in person. I scanned the room and located a woman dressed in a Chicago Bears sweatshirt. Sexy Body had obviously dialed the wrong e-mail address.

This could be fun.

Between periods of instruction, class members were free to investigate electronic bulletin boards and download useful materials. We could also practice sending e-mail. My brain nearing information-overload, I chose the latter option, feeling a little like I was passing notes in class.

During the afternoon break I sidled up to the mystery woman. "Are you single?" I asked.

"Yes, why?"

"I'm playing Cyrano De Bergerac."

"You're what?"

"I'm setting you up with the guy at the end of the second row."

She glanced over at him and giggled. "Go for it."

To make a long story shorter, four very tired, but very excited educators returned to the Peninsula that Friday evening pumped up with new and valuable knowledge. When the Internet connects with Hilltop Elementary, we'll be a little more able to guide our students safely through the maze of on-ramps to obtain world-wide access.

And as for Sexy Body and Little Chicago? I have a sneaking suspicion they'll be meeting up again real soon.

On the Road Again...

Sixth graders are awesome creatures. And just when you think you've figured out what kind of creatures they are, they turn on you like a chameleon.

Last Friday was the annual sixth grade field trip. I looked forward to it for weeks—just like I look forward to a trip to the dentist. Three hundred sixty four days a year I really like my dentist, and I'm genuinely fond of my sixth graders. But there's that one day when you wake up and wonder if it might not be a good idea to pull the covers up over your head and go back to sleep.

Only in my case I hadn't slept. Details had danced through my head all night. What if my alarm doesn't go off? (*I set two.*) What if my parent and grandparent helpers back out? (*They didn't.*) What if a child gets bus sick all over me? (*Not once so far.*) Silly little details that nonetheless kept me tossing and turning.

I boarded one of three buses loaded with precious cargo at 6:40 a.m. and reminded myself that no matter what happened, it would all be over in 10 hours. Ten fun-filled, action-packed, nerve-racking hours.

About eighty miles into the trip it occurred to me that it was awfully quiet in the back half of the bus. I mentioned that to a parent chaperone. "Want me to go back and stir them up?" he volunteered. He was too eager. I gave him my best 'do it and die' teacher look.

The bus driver, eyes ever scanning, told me that

nearly half the students were involved with some sort of battery-operated entertainment device, from portable CD players to a variety of electronic games. She used the microphone to request a child lower a potentially hazardous antenna. Loud groans erupted from the students in that vicinity.

"What are you using an antenna for?" I asked.

"We're watching T.V."

television?! They brought along a portable television?! Silly me. I'd thought the ultimate car toys were still Etch-a-sketch and magnetic checkers.

Our field trip had two parts. Part one was a viewing of "The Grand Canyon" film in Portland's OMNIMAX theatre. There we were told that the films for this domed theatre are over two and a half miles long, and are run through a two million dollar projector weighing over a ton. A forklift sets the projector in place once it is loaded.

Watching this sensory-encompassing film can be roughly equated to a) strapping oneself to the front of a raft to shoot the Colorado River rapids and b) clinging to the wing of a small plane while the ground repeatedly drops out from under you as the plane careens haphazardly through a maze of jagged rock formations and cliffs. It's not for the timid.

During lunch I pondered how well the second part of the trip would be received by these techno-preteens. Part two was a visit to the Portland Performing Arts Center and a demonstration by the Jefferson Dancers.

The Performing Arts Center is magnificent in its tasteful design. Mauve and teal are the predominant colors of the thick carpets, plush seats, velvet curtains and patterned wallpaper. The handrails are gleaming brass. We had a spectacular view from the first five rows of the balcony.

The Jefferson Dancers are high school students from all over Portland who have made a commitment to studying dance. They are bused to Jefferson High for a daily hour and a half instruction class in the afternoon and rehearse for two hours each day after school.

We saw them perform ballet, jazz, the tango, rumba, and tap. A few 'street dancing' techniques were thrown in during the improvisational portions of their routine. Each time the spotlights dimmed, our group of 130 responded with enthusiastic applause.

One of the highlights of my near-perfect day came when the girl sitting in front of me turned around and whispered, "Isn't this music from 'Porgy and Bess?'"

"Yes," I nodded, and said a silent prayer for parents everywhere who regularly provide culturally enriching experiences for their children.

Another highlight came as I waited back at Hilltop for the last few students to be picked up. "What was your favorite part of the whole trip?" I asked a boy dressed in a hat and coat sporting NBA logos.

Instantly, his face lit up. He made a quick check to see who was listening. "The tap dancers," he confided. "They were awesome."

How I Spent My Summer Vacation

Raise your hand if you got any sleep last night. Go ahead—don't be bashful—you won't be graded on this. But if that's your hand waving so alertly in the air, I'll venture that you're not a student, or a parent, or a teacher, or have anything at all to do with public education on the peninsula.

Today is the first day of school, and I'll bet a whole box of number two pencils that last night could only be rivaled by Christmas Eve for collective sleeplessness in our community.

Remember how you felt as a child the night before school started? The butterflies that couldn't be stilled deep in the pit of your stomach? Now we call it anxiety—that feeling of uncertainty or uneasiness about the future—but as kids, we were just plain worried.

What if I miss the bus? Will I be wearing the "right" clothes? How do I sign up for hot lunch? When do we get to go to the bathroom? Where *is* the bathroom? Will any of my friends be in my class? Will there be a lot of homework? What if I get a mean teacher? (*Now hold it right there—all together, how many truly mean teachers did you come across in your entire academic career?*)

And then there was that dreaded first day of school essay to look forward to. What business was it of the teachers' to ask about your summer, anyway?

Of course, now that we're adults (*at least chronologically*), we know that the teacher was only trying to evaluate our current abilities by obtaining a writing sample. Our spelling, sentence structure, ability to form paragraphs, even our critical thinking skills were graphically displayed by how legibly we wrote on the lines.

Essays aside, my memories of elementary school are highly positive ones. When I hear a bell ring in September—any bell—my mind returns to images of billowing chalk dust as we beat the erasers each recess, and the lingering smell of freshly inked purple dittos. (*Now of course, we have "dustless" chalk, and handouts are reproduced on a black line copier.*) I even enjoyed the supposed hassle of shopping for new school clothes.

Times have changed. No longer do students have separate "school clothes" and "play clothes." Computer games beat out reading a book by more than 10 to 1 for leisure activity time spent. Drug and alcohol awareness is now part of the regular school curriculum. By the age of 10, less than half the students are living with both of their biological parents.

Yes, things are different than when we were in school, but there's no reason to be discouraged. The most critical factor of academic success is still a constant. A current radio and television commercial, sponsored by the National Education Association (NEA) says it best: "Show me a parent who truly cares about a child's education, and I'll show you a child who can learn."

Parents—please, please, please— be involved in your children's education. Ask about their day at school—*every day*. Assist with homework. Review together the corrected papers brought home—all of them—even the ones that don't have an "A" on the top. Praise your students for trying hard. Attend conferences, Open House, and special programs. If your work schedule permits, volunteer in the classroom—even an hour a week is appreciated by the teachers, and it sends a tangible message to your child. Above all, show your children that education is important. Show them you truly care.

Okay, I'll put my soapbox away now. I've got a stack of essays to read tonight, and then I think it'll be about time to try to get a little sleep. It's going to be a great year.

Home Ec 101: Cooking Class

Home Economics was one of the electives available to ninth graders when I attended Lynnwood Junior High. The choices were Home Ec, Art or Band.

All the band kids had started playing their instruments in the fifth or sixth grades. All the art kids already *knew* how to draw a three-dimensional cube. All the rest of us signed up for Home Ec.

The first semester my group was assigned to the cooking lab. Our teacher, I believe her name was Miss Stackulson, tried her darnedest to teach us the "proper" way to do each kitchen task. Time and again she reprimanded us with the simple admonition, "Did you ever think there might be a better way to do it?"

Miss S.'s well-meaning phrase became a standard junior high joke, guaranteed to get a laugh whenever and wherever it was used: In other classrooms, the hallways, the gym, the cafeteria, ad infinitum.

Thinking about it now, Miss Stackulson must have been a first year teacher. Absolutely everything she did was "by the book." Rule number one dictated that what we cooked, we ate. And since Home Ec was the period right after lunch, most of us pocketed our lunch money on cooking days and happily ate the concoctions we created.

This arrangement wasn't too bad when we fixed muffins or grilled cheese sandwiches, but when we had to include broccoli in our menu to satisfy food group requirements and prepare tomato soup from scratch, some of the group balked.

"What kind of a teacher would threaten to flunk a kid who doesn't happen to like broccoli?" asked Denise, angrily sticking her fork through a "tender crisp" vegetable spear and waving it in the air. (*It may be noted here that the veggie was certainly more "crisp" than "tender."*)

"Girls! Girls!" said Miss S., hastening to our kitchen team. "You don't *stab* it, you *poke* it!" And she demonstrated (*with a fork she carried in her apron pocket for just these occasions*) what she considered to be the only acceptable method for getting broccoli from one's plate to one's mouth.

"Did you ever think," whispered Denise as soon as Miss S. was safely out of earshot, "that there might be a better way to do it?" And then she zeroed in on another broccoli spear, flinging it deftly from her fork to the nearby garbage can.

Half the class laughed their lunch right up their noses.

"Well I don't care *what* she says," said Dot. "If I have to eat this tomato soup, I'll puke." She resolutely set her spoon next to the bowl.

"Who ever heard of making tomato soup from a 'medium white sauce'?" asked Denise. "Hasn't she ever heard of the Campbell soup company?"

"No kidding." I agreed. "And with Jiffy muffin mixes, you just add eggs and water. I don't see why we have to reinvent the wheel."

Denise nodded thoughtfully while she munched on a saltine. "At least we didn't have to make our own soup crackers."

Miss S. reappeared at our table. She instructed Dot to eat every single bite of her tomato soup or none of us would be dismissed to our next class on time.

Dot, bless her heart, looked sadly around the group, shrugged, picked up the spoon and wolfed it down. And then Dot, bless her heart, proved to all of us that she was a woman of her word.

I'll never forget the look on Miss Stackulson's face when Dot pushed her chair back, stood up, clutched her stomach, emitted a pitiful little cry, and spewed the most beautiful light pink fountain high into the air. A cotton candy-colored mist fell upon the table, chairs, textbooks, notebooks, and several slower classmates.

After that we referred to Dot as "Old Faceful." And after that, it was no longer a requirement of the class to eat *everything* we cooked, although Miss Stackulson still insisted we take a small taste of unfamiliar foods.

I catch myself thinking about Miss S. every now and then as I take my microwave dinner from the kitchen to the rec room to watch television while I eat. Miss S. would not approve. Miss S. thought the dining room table should be set with placemats, matching cloth napkins and full silver for every meal—even if you're dining alone.

And sometimes I *do* set the dining room table (*when I can get one end of it cleared off*) and dine by candlelight. And at times like that I wish Miss S. was right there with me.

'Cause after the meal is over, *someone* has to do all those dishes…

Home Ec 102: Sewing Class

Jeanne won the Golden Seam-Ripper Award for the term; Barb was a close second. I know I was somewhere in the running, but I was too busy coordinating the sewing machine foot pedal races to worry about losing out on the glory.

As if first semester junior high home ec wasn't disastrous enough, the same group of ninth graders traversed across the hall from cooking lab to sewing lab for the second half of the year.

Miss Stackulson, ever the trooper, passed out a vocabulary list the first day of class. Until then, I thought *yardage* was something you got on a football field and *bias* was what Martin Luther King, Jr. spoke so eloquently against.

We had three project assignments that term: A draw-string gym bag, an A-line skirt, and an A-line dress. Heaven help us.

My first trip to the fabric store I picked out a nice Kelly green piece of durable-looking material for my gym bag. The sales clerk unrolled the bolt of cloth and picked up the scissors.

"Wait!" I told her, suddenly panicked. "You better double it—I might make a mistake."

But I didn't make a mistake. The gym bag only required two straight side-seams and a machine sewn "hem" for the drawstring. I decided to use the leftover gym bag material for the second project. The skirt, however, required following a specific pattern that included darts, waistband facing, a seven-inch zipper and a hand-sewn hem.

"Do you want me to double the yardage?" asked the fabric store clerk on my third trip in. "This material has to be cut carefully or it has a tendency to unravel." She wasn't kidding; it took me hours to get it right.

And from there it was all downhill. By the time I got the pattern cut out correctly I was a little behind the rest of the class. By the time I got the sewing machine threaded, I was quite a bit behind the rest of the class. By the time I got matching thread onto a bobbin, I was so far behind the rest of the class I resorted to taking shortcuts.

"Why should I waste time basting in the darts?" I asked Jeanne. "What can possibly go wrong?"

And by not basting the darts in first, I became the only class member to sew skirt darts on the *outside* of the skirt. Today it might have started a fashion trend; back then it wasn't one bit funny.

In the following weeks, I couldn't get the facing to lie flat, the zipper got sewn in upside-down, and the hem puckered and pulled until it looked like the skirt had a ruffle on the bottom.

"Every stitch you stitch on Monday," said Barb, misquoting the old proverb, "you'll take out with your nose on Tuesday and Wednesday and Thursday and Friday."

Barb was correct: I took out five times more stitches than I left in each week.

Knowing other girls in the class were having similar problems was a small comfort. I began having nightmares. It was me against machine. I awoke in a cold sweat, imagining my fingers all stitched together, sporting rows of bloody perforations with broken bobbin threads sticking out every which way.

The third project loomed between me and a passing grade. When backed into a corner, I can be quite resourceful. I knew that Mrs. Hagstrom, a woman I often babysat for, enjoyed sewing. By bartering with babysitting time, I convinced her to help me complete my dress before the end of the term.

And I vowed never to go near a sewing machine again—a promise I've been able to keep without effort.

So what became of the infamous Seam-Ripper Queens? Well, sad to say, I lost track of Jeanne a few years after high school. But runner-up Barb qualifies for the "Local Girl Makes Good" award.

Barb lives in rural Montana. When it came time for her to dress her first child, she couldn't find the type of clothing she wanted. So Barb bought a second-hand sewing machine and made some baby clothing herself. Pretty soon other young mothers in the neighborhood asked where they could purchase outfits like the ones her infant wore.

You can guess the rest. Her income last year was in six figures.

As for me, I still can't sew a button on straight or put in a decent hem. But there's nothing I can't mend with Velcro and duct tape.

Change is Good

With a large, hinged, wooden compass and a few industrial strength jumbo rubber bands, I demonstrated how the muscles in the arm expand and contract. Soon 28 energetic fourth graders were busy flexing and comparing their biceps.

"Hey, Ms. B.!" one girl called out. "My dad says the strongest muscles in our bodies is the muscle in our butts."

The room noise diminished a few decibels. Most of the students looked toward me to observe my reaction. I opened my mouth to gently correct her when a classmate beat me to it.

"Geez, Nora," Brett said disgustedly, "don'tcha know you're not supposed to say that 'b-word' in school? You're supposed to say 'rear end'."

"Or 'fanny'," interjected another boy.

"My mom calls it my 'gluteus maximus'," said a second girl.

Brett's eyes nearly popped from his head. He waved his hand frantically in the air. "Ms. B.! Ms. B.!" he blurted out. "Does gluteus maximus really mean…" He pointed to his backside.

"Pretty much." I nodded. "And now, class, can we please get back to our discussion about biceps and triceps?"

"Wait!" hollered Brett. "That can't be!"

"Brett," I said calmly, "whatever is the matter?"

"Well, my mom sometimes calls me her little

'gluteus maximus cranius'. So, is she really saying I'm a little—"

"Fanny-head!" shrieked Nora, delighted with this new information. "Just like in 'Beevus and Fanny-head'!"

* * *

Recalling this typical classroom exchange makes me feel a bit nostalgic. Not teary-eyed—these kinds of stories always make me laugh—but definitely nostalgic. There are some very enjoyable things I'm going to miss about teaching fourth grade science. And math. And social studies. And art. And music. And P.E. And computers. And reading. And English. And spelling. And, well, I'm going to miss most everything there is about teaching in the intermediate grades.

Except maybe field trips. I was never too crazy about field trips.

But 'crazy' is exactly what those near and dear to me have been saying about my latest career move. The decision did not come without serious thought; I've been considering expanding my professional horizons for several years. And this year the perfect opportunity presented itself at the perfect time.

After 21 successful years teaching in grades three through six, I wholeheartedly accepted the challenge of seventh grade social studies and language arts.

"Seventh grade!" exclaimed my long-time friend Anna Marie. "Do you, by any chance, remember what you were like in seventh grade?!"

"I'm sure I'll behave more maturely now."

"I wasn't actually talking about *you*, and you know it! I was referring to those pre-pubescent hormones-on-legs wandering the hallways of the junior high school."

I smiled. "I'm excited about the change. It's going

to be fun."

"Fun?!" Anna Marie shook her head in disbelief. "Masochistic is more like it. Next thing I know, you'll be telling me you also enjoy having dental work done."

Poor Anna Marie. She'll never understand the unsurpassed rush of adrenalin I feel each fall when I hear the ringing of the school bell. It's a rush I've felt every September for the last 38 years. *Thirty-eight years!*

And now, for the first time since 1966, I'll be entering a classroom chock full of seventh graders. And believe it or not, I can hardly wait!

In preparation for the social studies portion of my assignment I spent the summer reading textbooks and writing lessons plans on Ancient Rome, Medieval Europe, The Crusades and The Renaissance (the latter of which I have finally learned to spell correctly). Although my college minor was history, it's been awhile since I've expounded upon the likes of King Arthur, Eleanor of Aquitaine, Richard the Lionhearted, Joan of Arc and Charlemagne (*which, incidentally, I also had to learn to spell!*).

I'm not worried about the language arts part. If I can teach Gray's Harbor College community education writing classes to senior citizens, 12 and 13 year olds ought to be a snap. (*Chill out, senior writers, I'm only kidding!*)

"Well," said Anna Marie, "I still think you're out of your mind, but at least now I know exactly what to get you for Christmas." She grinned mischievously. "By then I figure you'll be just about ready for a straitjacket."

It was my turn to grin. "Buy locally," I said, "and save the receipt."

"Are you that sure you'll be exchanging it in January?"

My smile turned to a hearty laugh. "You can bet your sweet gluteus maximus on it."

CHAPTER EIGHT
Critters

In Pursuit of the Mighty Mallard

Every year around the third week in January, right about the end of duck season, I find myself thinking about a man I knew in college. He was smart, funny, and had an absolute obsession about duck hunting.

"Must you spend every single weekend hunting ducks?" I naively asked him early in our relationship.

"The ducks don't care what day it is," he said as he reloaded shotgun shells. "Besides, I have classes all week."

"I was merely thinking how nice it would be to spend some quality time with you."

"The season only lasts from October until a few weeks after Christmas. We can have quality time then."

It was early November. If this relationship had a snowball's chance of surviving the holidays, I'd have to take drastic action.

"I could go hunting with you," I said softly.

And so I plunged headlong into a world of camouflage clothing, duck blinds, decoys, boats and purebred retrievers. If I'd known then what I know now...heck, I'd have probably done it anyway.

The typical weekend started as soon as classes

dismissed on Friday. We loaded his station wagon with sleeping bags, rain gear, boots and dog food, hitched on the boat, picked up his yellow Lab, and headed out to rendezvous at some remote eastern Washington reservoir with his dad and a couple other hunting buddies.

His dad had a camper. Sleeping in the camper was probably better than trying to sleep in the back of the station wagon with the Labrador. Probably. But then, maybe the dog didn't snore.

Somewhere in the vicinity of 4 or 5 a.m. we stumbled groggily to the boat, laden with every conceivable "necessity" and several thermoses of hot black coffee. After a short ride upriver, down river, or around the edge of the pothole, we began placing decoys.

By daybreak the decoys were all set, the boats were hidden under layers of netting among the reeds, and we were safely sequestered in the nearby blinds.

Daybreak was my favorite time. Being east of the Cascades, rain was rare, and the sunrises spectacular. The black and white pre-dawn became a rosy pink and the sagebrush covered hills were the perfect backdrop for an all blue kaleidoscope as the sky lightened. The still water reflected the few puffy white clouds and the cattails along the shore took on a golden glow. No place or time has ever felt more tranquil.

Until the first shot was fired. And the second, and the third, and the fourth, until the echoes reverberated back from the far cliffs and I felt like an auditory observer of "The Charge of the Light Brigade."

When the smoke cleared the dogs were sent out to retrieve whatever had been shot down among the decoys.

This same scene played out several times during the morning hours, interrupted only by an occasional request for more sandwiches or coffee. By early afternoon the duck calls fell silent as the hunters napped in their blinds.

So much for quality time.

Once while the men slept I took one of the dogs and went exploring. I crested a hill and discovered a large herd of elk feeding in the next dale. I would have been content to sit and watch for hours, but the dog thought it would be great sport to run among them. The elk opted to travel on.

Meanwhile, back at the blinds, it was nearing time for the evening shoot. Just prior to nightfall the ducks returned to roost in the reeds, and if they made an appearance while it was still light enough, they were fair game. But fair is fair, and often we were packing up for the night before any feathered fowl ventured within range. They'd be there another day.

Saturday night camp was spent cleaning ducks and poking fun at the hunters who missed their shots. When I think about it now, it was a "guy time," and I was somewhat of an intruder. Yet I always felt welcome, and I'm thankful for the times I went along.

My college friend is married now, with three lovely daughters. I hope they've been able to accompany Dad on a few hunting trips. True sportsmen (*and women*) know that time spent among the flora and fauna teaches genuine appreciation for nature's beauty as well as bounty. It's a lesson we all need to learn.

But I still think he could have skipped a weekend every now and then.

The Ants Go Marching Two by Two…

"Why so glum?" asked Anna Marie. "What's bugging you?"

"Interesting word choice." I sighed. "I can't put it off any longer; I gotta call Dennis."

"Dennis?!" Anna Marie leaned forward, her eyebrows arched with interest. "You haven't told me about a new man in your life!"

"He's not a 'new' man; I've known him for years."

"And you've kept him a secret?!"

"For crying out loud, Anna Marie, let me finish a sentence. Dennis is my pest exterminator."

"Uh-oh…" she settled back in her chair, "if you're on a first name basis with your exterminator, it must be serious."

It was.

In the beginning I'd tried to ignore them—the random ant here and there every day or two. *Just traveling through*, I told myself. *Don't panic. They're not moving in.* But I didn't believe it.

I've competed for living space with mice, possums, chipmunks, deer, bears, bats, bees, mosquitoes, fleas, spiders and an assortment of other 'critters' out here on the wild and woolly Sandridge Road. Most of the time it's an amicable co-habitation; they stay outside and I stay inside. It's when the boundaries are crossed that trouble brews.

Ants, from my observations, come in four sizes:

small, as in sugar ants; medium, as in sidewalk ants; large, as in carpenter ants; and jumbo, as in those nasty B-52 flying bombers.

The large ants are the ones I fear most—the kind that destroy a wooden structure from the inside out. *Just a few loners who lost their way*, I tried to convince myself.

But late one night I heard a raspy sound coming from inside a bedroom wall. I pulled the pillow over my head, but worry amplified the sound. I got up and pounded on the paneling. The noise got louder.

Trapped inside a wall, rodents will scratch, gnaw and claw their way out. This did not sound like scratching, gnawing, or clawing. This noise sounded like singing.

I recognized the tune from "Rawhide:"

"MUNCHING, MUNCHING, MUNCHING,
WE'RE SO BUSY LUNCHING,
IN THE WALLS WE'RE CRUNCHING,
SAW-DUST!"

"How long before they eat a whole house?" I asked Dennis when he arrived for an inspection.

"They don't eat wood, they nest in it," he patiently explained. "If they ate the wood, you wouldn't see any sawdust, like that pile there." He pointed to the spot where the living room wall adjoined the garage.

My stomach tied itself into an ugly knot.

"Before I spray," said Dennis, "you need to put away all foodstuffs. Put your canisters in the refrigerator. Seal everything else in zip-lock bags. Afterwards, you'll need to clean all food preparation surfaces and wash all dishes and silverware."

I'd have to wash *everything* in the kitchen? *Everything?* Didn't this man realize that I have 23 cupboards and 16 drawers in that room and all of them are crammed full of absolutely necessary items ranging from a bazillion cookie cutters to a wok I use every five years? Never mind that I don't *choose* to cook very often. When I *do* cook, it takes every pot, pan, mixing bowl and cookie sheet in the house. And now he wanted me to clean them without ever getting them visibly dirty?

My obsessive/compulsive tendencies kicked right straight into overdrive. "What about the cupboard shelves?" I asked him. "And the blender? The can opener? The coffeemaker? The waffle iron? The crockpot?

"The wine glasses, of course, and the wine rack that holds them, because if I touched the rack and then the glass it would be contaminated again. But what about the wine bottles themselves? And then there's the telephone to wipe off, the door knobs, the light switches, the remote control. *Yes, the remote control!* Hypothetically, I could sit down to eat an apple while watching TV and..."

I was beginning to sound silly, even to myself.

"Just wash the countertops a few hours after I leave," said the ever-patient Dennis, "rinse off the dishes before you use them , and there shouldn't be any problem."

Easy for him to say. Some of my dishes I only use once or twice a year. By Christmas I'd have forgotten which were washed and which weren't.

I decided to do the only reasonable thing; I packed up the entire kitchen and put everything in my car. Some people have 'Meals on Wheels;' for a few days last week I had an 'Auto-Mobile Kitchenette.'

Now the only thing bugging me is paying good money for dead ants. But it sure beats living in my car.

Camping Out

Here it comes: The long awaited Fourth of July Weekend. The weekend where, traditionally, the mountain people go to the beach; the beach people go to the mountains; the city people go to the country; and the country people wish they didn't have to stick close enough to home to milk the cows twice a day.

On a long summer weekend like this, most everyone wants to pack up his/her troubles in his/her old kit bag and go somewhere else—most everyone, that is, except me.

I'm quite content to hang out here at the beach. During the day I'll get to meet a lot of nice people as I hawk my books with other 'art and crafters' in the Ocean Park school gym. After festival hours, I plan to spend my evenings kicking back with a few cold beverages while waiting for the sky to be dark enough to wave some safe and sane sparklers.

But a few of my well-meaning friends think I'm in danger of becoming an old stick-in-the-mud fuddy-duddy.

"You really should get out more," said Anna Marie. "Come camping with us. You'll have a ball. We've got reservations in a great park near Lake Wenatchee."

"I don't camp."

"Jan, this is Anna Marie you're talking to. If I recall correctly, and I'm pretty sure I do, when you were a kid your family used to take weekend mini-vacations in a trailer to places all over Eastern Washington."

"Don't remind me." I shuddered. "Two adults and four kids crammed into an 18-foot thermos bottle with no privacy, no real bathroom, no hot showers, no electricity hook-ups and no foreseeable way out. No thank you."

"You won't be crammed into a trailer with us—we're tent camping."

"You've got to be kidding. The last time I slept on the ground I had body parts hurting for days that I previously didn't even know existed." I managed a rueful smile. "Why does everyone have all these romanticized notions about camping out, anyway?"

"We're communing with nature."

"If you had cable TV you could watch National Geographic from the comfort of your favorite recliner."

"We'll be singing camp songs and roasting marshmallows."

"I'll be channel-surfing and eating microwaved popcorn."

"Come on, be a good sport…"

"Aren't you the least bit afraid of bears? A few years ago a friend of mine had a rather brazen black bear rip a hole in her tent while she was taking a moonlight swim in Lake Chelan. Seems he was after her half-empty coffee cup. Imagine what might have happened if she'd been inside the tent when this bear got his sudden craving for caffeine."

"Honestly, Jan…"

"I've said it before, and I'll say it again: My idea of roughing it is a black and white TV in the Holiday Inn."

"Oh, pigeon poop!" retorted Anna Marie.

"Speaking of pigeons," I said, "the last time I was at Lake Wenatchee, what I thought were friendly flocks of small birds turned out to be swarms of underfed and overly-aggressive mosquitoes. And while mosquitoes don't poop on my head, I've never before had a pigeon suck my blood, either."

Anna Marie shook her head. "If you decide to change your mind..."

"I won't. But I'll send along some calamine lotion and my last bottle of raspberry schnapps...for medicinal purposes only, of course."

Before Anna Marie's mouth could form the question, I continued, "Ever hear of rattlesnakes?"

"Bears, mosquitoes, rattlesnakes," said Anna Marie, "what's with this unilateral rejection of wildlife?"

"It's not that I dislike wildlife," I replied. "It's just that I prefer to spend my Fourth of July Weekend with the wildlife out on the beach during the fireworks."

"I give up," said Anna Marie. "We're going without you."

"That's fine. You can say 'hello' to Yogi and Boo-boo for me."

"Yogi and Boo-boo live in *Jellystone Park*," said Anna Marie, getting in the last word. "I told you you should get out more—your geography's getting rusty. Not even in the cartoons is Lake Wenatchee *anywhere near* Yellowstone Park."

Anna Marie was right about that. And although I hate to admit it, she was right about me getting out more too. The real Yellowstone National Park, with its multi-colored geysers and hot springs, plethora of animals and spectacular panoramic vistas actually sounds like a pretty good idea.

I wonder if they have a Motel 6...

Not a Creature was Stirring

Rasputin cleared his throat. A small colony of gray mice huddled close about him. "I'm afraid I have some bad news," he began.

A twitter of concern passed through the assembly. Every eye and every ear turned in his direction as a hush fell among them.

"Our faithful friend and trusty scout Horatio was killed last evening."

The murmurs turned to gasps of disbelief and sobs of despair.

"His family has been notified," continued Rasputin. "The memorial service will be held day after tomorrow."

In the silence that followed, Timothy asked the question in everyone's mind. "How did he die, Rasputin? Can you give us any details?"

"You all know what a good provider Horatio was," said Rasputin. "He had been working overtime all last month to make sure his children would have a festive celebration with plenty of holiday food for their big banquet..."

Rasputin stopped to blow his nose. Wiping his trembling whiskers, he steadied his voice. "The bottom line is, well, the bottom line is that his sweet tooth got the best of him."

"Sweet tooth?" asked Timothy. "I don't understand..."

"Horatio was overly fond of sweets: Candy, cake, pie, you name it, he loved noshing on goodies of all kinds. Early last night he was scoping out that green house halfway down the block when he discovered a counter top lined with several hundred pieces of cashew candy.

"Now, Horatio figured nobody would miss just one little piece, so, even though the people in the house had not yet retired for the night, he pulled a single nut cluster back behind the microwave to sample.

"Unfortunately, when the candy maker returned to the kitchen, she *did* notice a piece of candy missing, and although Horatio ducked behind the wine rack, she was none too pleased to have a rodent, however cute and cuddly, running amuck among her canisters—

"To put it mildly, she screamed bloody murder."

"But how did he die?" persisted Timothy.

"After securing the candy in airtight containers and stashing them in the refrigerator, the woman got out her entire barrage of mousetraps, eight in all, and placed them strategically around the perimeter of the counter top, leaving the nibbled nugget in plain sight as an extra enticement."

"But surely Horatio had avoided traps in that house before," said Timothy. "After all, he was the one who warned us when she brought home those pesky cats last month... What made him careless?"

"You're not going to like this," said Rasputin. "But this particular candy maker decided to bait her traps with..." He paused, surveying the group before him.

"With what?!" Timothy's tail twitched agitatedly.

Rasputin sighed deeply. "With... cheesecake."

"Cheesecake?!" The entire colony erupted into fits of indignation.

"Is that legal?" asked Timothy, when he could make

himself heard above the emotional outpouring of the crowd.

"Humans don't always play fair," replied Rasputin quietly.

"Let's go gnaw through all her electrical cords!" cried one mouse.

"Let's chew her leather shoes!" yelled another.

"Let's leave droppings on her toothbrush!"

"Let's build a nest in the middle of her jumbo box of Costco toilet tissue!"

Rasputin held up his paws for silence. "Quiet everyone! Please! Quiet!"

Timothy elbowed the mouse next to him. "I'll bet Rasputin already has a plan," he whispered. "Listen..."

"Beginning today, there's going to be a few mandated dietary changes around here—"

"Dietary changes?" asked an incredulous Timothy, not sure he had heard correctly. "Horatio gets killed and he wants to put us all on a *diet?*"

"Effective immediately," continued Rasputin, "no mouse shall partake of any form of non-regulation food goody. For the health and welfare of the entire colony, it shall be unlawful to partake of anything but the basics. If we strengthen our resolve to stick to the grains, pine nuts, bread crumbs, cheese in small quantities, etc., we should all be able to make it through the rest of the winter without any additional misfortune."

"Rasputin!" exclaimed Timothy, "is this your response to Horatio's untimely death, or the fact that you've been gaining a few pounds during the holidays?"

"Ulterior motives not withstanding," replied the ever-honest Rasputin, "for Horatio's demise not to be in vain, we need to learn from his experience. As the new year begins, I want you all to remember the moral of Horatio's tragic story."

"And what might that be?" Timothy asked sarcastically.

"The moral is," concluded Rasputin, "that if you think *just one bite* of cheesecake won't kill you...think again!"

Having Kittens

Saturday afternoon I got a phone call from a woman I'll call Mrs. X. Mrs. X and her family own a home on Sandridge Road. She calls herself a "weekender."

Mrs. X called me because she reads this column, thought we might be neighbors, and didn't know where else to turn. Mrs. X had a problem.

Sometime during the last month, a soon-to-be Mama Cat crawled under the tarp on the X's boat looking for a warm, dry place to have her litter. Four small kittens had been found inside the cabin when the X's 16-year-old daughter climbed in to clean it out for the summer boating season.

"What can I do?" asked Mrs. X. "We haven't seen the Mama Cat, and it's been hours since we discovered the kittens. We're moving the boat, so they can't stay in there, and I can't take them back to our place in the city. Who can I call?"

Who, indeed?

The Blue Sawhorse is a thrift shop located at 504 N. Pacific. Their receipts provide help to animals in need. They disperse emergency pet food, and give financial assistance for a pet's medical concerns. They are not, and cannot be, an animal shelter.

"We used to have 'foster homes' for pets waiting to be 'adopted'," says Jan Barney at The Blue Sawhorse, "but now the best we can offer is a spot on our bulletin board advertising the pet needing a home."

Oceanside Animal Clinic is requested to "put down" over 300 unwanted, but otherwise healthy animals, each year. "We try to find other options," says Catherine Lindblad, veterinarian, "but the Peninsula has reached the super-saturation point with cats."

What about the Humane Society? We have one, but it's essentially in name only until they get enough donations with which to complete a shelter.

So what was Mrs. X supposed to do? If she took them to the vet, she would be assuming responsibility (*financial and emotional*) for the disposition of the four tiny kittens. If she left them in a laundry basket on her back porch, there was a chance Mama Cat would return for them, but no guarantee.

A third option was unthinkable.

Hundreds of feral cats are living in the woods of the Peninsula. Some of the jerks that dump their pets actually think they're doing them a favor by turning them loose, saying "at least I didn't shoot the kittens, or drown them, or hit them in the head with a shovel." They rationalize that this way the cats or kittens get a fighting chance.

Yeah, right. So how many of those six-week-old kittens fight their way out of a gunnysack only to become coyote snacks?

What dumping a cat in the woods really does is create a problem for someone with more common sense, as well as compassion. Someone like Mrs. X.

While kittens may be the cutest and cuddliest balls of fluff you've ever seen, sooner of later they will be old enough to breed. And when that happens, the responsible thing to do is to have it spayed or neutered. Plan for this before you ever bring a pet into your home.

No excuses.

If money is an issue, The Blue Sawhorse, in cooperation with Oceanside, attempts to run a free or reduced clinic twice a year. Appointments are booked until the money runs out. The next one, donations permitting, will be in August.

And speaking of donations, The Blue Sawhorse, mailing address P.O. Box 1047, Long Beach, accepts dog or cat food, and money in any amount, to continue to promote animal welfare on the Peninsula. The money they collect is put to immediate use.

For a long-range solution, in the form of a full-time animal shelter, the Humane Society's address is c/o Milt Wadler, P.O. 418, also in Long Beach.

As for Mrs. X, the Mama Cat did show up, some 9 or 10 hours later, and carried her children, one by one, off into the dark of night. A happy ending?

You decide.

**NOTE: The current address of the community-supported no-kill South Pacific Count Humane Society is P.O. 101, Long Beach, WA 98631. Donations are always welcome!*

Flash Cat

"Did you stop out at the barn?" asked Pat as I entered her kitchen.

"Uh-huh."

"Well, did you see the kitten?"

"I told you, I don't want another cat."

"That's not what I asked." She smiled and handed me a cup of coffee.

"All I saw in the barn was a flash—just a quick blond flash as the kitten darted behind a bale of hay."

"Flash?" she asked coyly. "If you've already named it, the kitten's yours."

But I didn't want another cat. In six years I'd buried four cats. In the unlikely event that I was *ever* to have another cat, I'd planned to name it 'Number Five.' If it was only a number, I reasoned, I might keep from getting so attached to it.

The blond flash in the barn was a long-haired, yellow-orange mixed breed, the son of a white tailless Manx and who knew what else. His sisters, all immediately placed in good homes, were gray stub-tails. The 'runt' of the litter, this golden boy's tail was a fluffy, full-length plume.

The kitten in question had one eye that frequently lost focus, causing him to look at me in the most beguiling cross-eyed manner. Leave it to me to be drawn to a cat in need of corrective lenses.

"You caught me in a moment of weakness," I said,

holding him for the first time seven and a half years ago. "My divorce just became final, and a cat might be a good idea after all. This little fella has a lot of personality; he'll be good company."

Pat raised an eyebrow.

"Don't look at me like that." I blushed. "The way I figure it, it's a fair trade—

"So what," I interrupted myself, "shall his middle name be? 'Dance' or 'Gordon?'"

Although born a barn cat, Flash was housebroken in three days. When he wanted to go out, he sat beside the back door and stared at it until I opened it. If he had to go out *really badly*, he scratched or squeaked. (*Having no role model, he never managed a realistic meow.*)

Supposedly, a cat is a low-maintenance pet. The first week Flash cost me a set of drapes, a lamp shade and three toes. One corner of the couch became his permanent scratching post.

"You can save yourself some money on cat food," the vet told me when I took Flash in for a thorough physical and a myriad of shots. "He can get all the nutrition he needs in dry food. If he's never introduced to canned food, he won't miss it."

She was right. Years later, when I neglected to bring home a new bag of cat food and offered him dinner from a can (*kept in the cupboard for emergencies*), he turned his nose up at it. Yet the vet wouldn't have approved of what Flash eventually ate that night.

Normally, Flash was an incredibly well-behaved animal. He learned early on that tables and counters were off limits. While I ate my dinner he often curled up on a nearby chair, but he was never, ever, fed table scraps. That's why it stunned me when he waited until I was busy in the kitchen, climbed up into *my* chair at the table and polished off *my* plate of burritos.

He had bad gas for a week.

His first Christmas Flash was mesmerized by the twinkling tree lights and the sparkling tinsel. I expected him to take a swipe or two at the bright balls on the lower branches.

Not Flash.

Flash took one long, flying leap into the center of the 12-foot tree and shimmied clear to the top, where he clung for dear life as the tree listed and teetered and finally toppled to the floor.

Temporarily pinned beneath the tree, he caterwauled like I was beating him senseless, which did, I admit, seem like a good idea at the time.

'They' say you can't train a cat, but Flash was no ordinary cat. He came running whenever I whistled for him, and he learned to roll over and play dead for a taste of his cod liver oil-based hairball medicine.

The only thing he never figured out was that he had to duck when he walked under the rungs of the dining room chairs. "K-thunk, k-thunk, k-thunk, k-thunk, k-thunk—" If he dashed beneath the table during our games of tag, he lost his advantage for a surprise attack. It must have had something to do with his double vision.

Flash disappeared Memorial Weekend. Unlike his predecessors, he left no trace. Each evening as I pull into the driveway I expect to see him yawn and stretch up on the woodshed roof before racing me to the back door. His food dish remains full.

This is it for me; it's the end of the 15-year omnipresent feline dynasty at my house. I won't have, I cannot bear, I do not want, another cat.

Yet.

Photo Opportunities with a Plexi-glassed Bear

"What's your excuse this time?" asked Anna Marie.

"I decided to run away and join the circus."

"What made you decide to do a thing like that on one of the two nights a week you've set aside to do some serious writing?"

"Listen, Anna Marie, I can sit at the keyboard any old time. The circus comes to town only once in a blue moon—I just couldn't pass it up."

"And why not?"

"It's a long story. It has something to do with the fact that when I was a kid I saw 'Toby Tyler' eight times."

"Let me get this straight," sighed Anna Marie. "Three decades ago you watched a circus movie and now suddenly, right when you should have been tackling chapter four of your new book, you felt compelled to go check out the trapeze artists."

"I saw the movie at a very impressionable age."

So what *really* made me drive over to Astoria on a windy and rainy March afternoon to sit for two and a half hours on cold metal bleachers? Was it merely another tactic in my long list of finely tuned procrastination techniques? Or do I still harbor a childhood fascination with the people and events found under the big top?

This was my first visit to the new Clatsop County Fairgrounds. Although the accommodations were adequate,

I was disappointed to discover I wouldn't be viewing the three make-shift rings inside a huge canvas tent. Some of the thrill was lost when the guy walking on the outside of the whirling 'Wheel of Destiny' had to duck to avoid hitting his head on the metal roof.

The circus organizers didn't miss a trick. Children under 12 were admitted free; accompanying adults paid nine dollars to attend. Parking was a dollar. Toys and trinkets for sale lined the walkway from the entrance gate to the grandstand.

Before the show and during intermission, tickets were sold for Shetland pony rides, elephant rides, and time to jump around in the inflated 'Moon Walk.' For a mere five dollars, parents could purchase a Polaroid picture of their happy child standing next to a lace-collared circus bear. The bear, however, was separated from the children by a thick acrylic barrier.

Hundreds of dollars exchanged hands as tiny tots begged for popcorn, cotton candy, cheese-covered nachos, pop and sno-cones—and that was just in the row where I was sitting.

(*Rumor has it that the amount of money spent on stomachache remedies later that evening far exceeded ticket sale receipts.*)

Oddly enough, no one was hawking hot dogs. And peanuts were another conspicuous omission; no peanut shells littered the ground. At first I assumed it had something to do with the arena's custodial maintenance contract, but maybe it was another ploy to increase the profit margin. Instead of real honest-to-goodness roasted legumes, clowns cruised the stands with 'Commemorative M&M Peanuts®,' which sold for a dollar per puny little box as a circus fund-raiser.

For those overflowing with miscellaneous food fare,

the ringmaster reminded the audience every few minutes that an assortment of balloons, battery-operated glow-in-the-dark rainbow wands and circus coloring books were still available in limited quantities to take home as event mementos.

"So," Anna Marie broke into my reverie, "was it worth skipping out on your writing schedule?"

I thought about the jugglers twirling fire batons, balancing on ladders, spinning barrels with their feet; the clowns doing classic vaudevillian shtick routines; the motorcyclists verifying the existence of centrifugal force inside a steel cage-like ball; the aerial acrobats, wearing not much more than sequins, dangling by their ankles high overhead.

I remembered the animal acts: the African lions and Siberian tigers, the dancing bears, the prancing horses and the trained Rottweiler dogs. I smiled as I recalled the five elephant grand finale. Why, the whole trip was worth it just to watch those colossal pachyderms perform.

"Yes," I nodded. "Going to the circus was absolutely, positively, beyond a shadow of a doubt, the best thing I could have done for myself that day."

"Then I have just one more question," said Anna Marie. She cleared her throat. "Next time you decide to run away for the afternoon…next time…will you take me with you?"

"Well, I don't know…," I hedged. "It seems to me that Toby Tyler didn't take a whole entourage with him when *he* ran away to join the circus…"

"I'll pay for the cotton candy."

"You're on."

CHAPTER NINE
Free Enterprise

Strawberry Fields Forever

"Incoming!" hollered 13-year-old Billy, just as a sloggy, mushy, overripe strawberry splatted against my cheek.

"Ow!" I yelled, much louder than necessary. Dramatically, I wiped the red juice and seedy residue from my face. "You're disgusting, Billy!"

The row boss instantly descended upon him. "Billy Webster!" She roughly grabbed his ear and pulled him to his feet. "Billy Webster, just for that I ought to make you pick the worst row in the field. How'd you like that?"

I knew she was bluffing; Billy and I were the best pickers she had. We always got the choice rows so she'd have prime berries to sell to people in cars who stopped along the highway.

"Aw, Mom…" said Billy. "Can't I just apologize?"

Mrs. Webster agreed, and Billy came over to solemnly shake my hand—the very hand in which I had just mashed up a fistful of rotten berries. As his hand connected with mine, I squished the pulp through his fingers. Billy grimaced, but to his credit, said nothing. He wiped his hand on the leg of his jeans and knelt back down to continue picking.

For three summers, Billy and I were arch enemies—bitter rivals. I've always enjoyed a little healthy competition, and even though Billy was a full year older, I gave him a run for his money when it came to claiming the title of "top picker" each week.

Mrs. Webster was the row boss. It was up to her to make sure each row was picked clean. If we missed too many ripe berries we had to go back and pick it over again, start to finish, while other kids got fresh rows to harvest. I learned fast to do it right the first time through.

Mrs. Webster also drove the berry bus. I sincerely don't know how she did it—there are times I'm sure we must have driven her just about mad.

At 6 a.m., six days a week, Mrs. Webster wheeled the bus up to the corner where we waited, lunch pails in hand, for the two and a half hour trip to the berry fields near Mount Vernon. The ride would have been much shorter, except we had to collect kids from stops in Lynnwood, Edmonds, Mountlake Terrace and Everett before we got to where we were going.

There was plenty of time to sing "99 Bottles of Beer on the Wall" from start to finish at least twice, along with "Found a Peanut," "The Ants Go Marching," and the ever-popular "We All Live in a Yellow Berry Bus."

Being one of the first on the bus, and therefore one of the last to get home, I often put in close to a 12 hour day. In the seven or eight hours actually in the field, I could pick six to eight flats of berries.

For each flat picked, the row boss punched the cards we wore pinned to our shirts. Each flat translated into 85¢. Twenty flats filled a card. At the end of the week, we turned our cards in when we arrived and got a paycheck as we boarded the bus to go home. My best week I picked 45 flats of berries and made almost $40. I was rich!

I was rich and I had a back so sore I could hardly stand up straight. A flat of berries was 12 quart boxes. *quarts*, not pints. The boxes had to be full to heaping before the row boss punched your ticket. Many times she'd take one of the 12 containers and dump it over the top of the other 11 boxes and then make you go back out and finish off the flat.

Fortunately, strawberry season lasted only five weeks. Unfortunately, since I was a good worker, I was invited to come back out and pick raspberries for another three or four weeks. At least there wasn't as much bending to do—but there WAS the little matter of the heavy wooden "belly bumpers" we wore tied with a rope around our waists to pick the berries into.

But nevertheless, we thought we were in heaven: Raspberries paid 95¢ a flat! And with every berry I picked, I knew I was just that much closer to paying my first year's college tuition.

Of course I didn't put every berry I picked into my flat. A few I saved to pelt Billy with when his mother wasn't looking: Raspberry bushes, I quickly discovered, provide a lot more cover than strawberry plants.

A Matter of National Security

There's nothing I love more than school clothes shopping. Each August, for the past (dare I say it?) 37 years, I've eagerly looked forward to climbing in and out of dozens of outfits, sorting through each and every fashion on countless racks searching for those that fit not too small, not too large, but just right. What joy! What bliss!

What a bunch of malarkey!

While some women (and a lesser number of men) can spend hours, days, or weeks on end cruising the malls, I've never been among that number. I figure there's a reason why *maladjusted, malicious, malignant* and *malls* all appear on the same dictionary page. Another reason I've never considered shopping a high-profile Olympic event is that my endurance for dealing with salesclerks is shamefully low.

But nevertheless, I consider myself a good sport. So when my friend Alice persuaded me to venture into the inner sanctum of a big-city department store, I (*albeit reluctantly*) agreed to stand half-naked in a small, sweaty dressing room while she brought me every garment within a 30 mile radius that looked like it might be in my size.

Unfortunately, Alice, bless her heart, has somewhat different clothing tastes than I do. By the end of the afternoon, my "gofer" had presented me with 437 outfits that I couldn't imagine wearing to my own funeral.

"Just try it on," cajoled Alice as my tolerance level

plummeted. "I bet you'll look cute."

Cute is not a word I've often used to describe myself. I've also had precious few friends who've had the patience to put up with my less-than-gracious shopping attitude. Therefore, it seemed only prudent to humor her.

And miracles do happen. Hours later, my hand shook as I signed the credit card receipt for four—yes four—dresses, the first I'd purchased in years. We emerged victorious from the relative cool of the store into the 95 degree August sunshine and proceeded homeward. But the adventure was just beginning...

"Alice," I said, modeling my new apparel in my living room that evening, "the salesclerk forgot to remove the plastic security tags from two of these dresses." I read the warning printed on the tag aloud, "Tampering with this device will emit ink into the fabric."

"Uh-oh," said Alice.

Uh-oh indeed.

Bright and early the next morning I called Directory Assistance for the number of the big-city department store. The second call got me to the store's main switchboard. The store operator gave me the number to dial Customer Service direct. Call number three connected me with a voice message which explained that the Customer Service office opened at 10 a.m.

It was 9:57.

I waited 10 minutes and dialed again. All Customer Service lines were currently busy, intoned the automated answering machine, but please hold on, and my call would be taken in the order it was received.

Ten minutes later I gave up and redialed the main switchboard. I got the number of the store manager. The store manager gave me the toll-free number of the Sensor-Matic company in Florida, who could tell me the nearest store where I could have the security tags removed.

The nice woman in Florida had me list all towns within three counties, along with their proper spellings, and their zip codes, if I happened to know them offhand.

Twenty-five minutes elapsed, during which I heard, between Muzak selections, that Sensor-Matic was a worldwide leader in security systems, responsible not only for the UPP (*Universal Process Program*) applied to clothing, but also food and pharmaceutical safeguards and the video surveillance at the 1996 Olympics.

All I wanted was to wear my new clothes.

At long last, a boutique in Seaside was identified as having the security removal apparatus needed. I thanked the woman and told her I had just one more question: Why hadn't the security system stopped me from leaving the Portland store? She gave me several possible explanations, but the bottom line was that I'd have to make a trip to Seaside to get the tags removed. "And don't forget to take your receipt with you," she advised.

Seven long-distance calls, an 80 mile round-trip to Seaside, and presto! all's well that ends well. Which brings me to the end of this column, and one final thought: Imagine, with no limitations whatsoever to your imaginings, how the course of American history might have been changed with ink-emitting security tags…

Ms. Tool Time

One crisp fall morning a little less than two weeks ago, an esteemed colleague breezed into my classroom toting a large cardboard carton.

"What's in the box?" I queried.

"The materials for making the name tags we'll need at the sixth grade retreat," she replied.

"Jo," I said patiently, "all I need to make name tags is a felt marker and a couple dozen index cards."

"Oh no, no, no, no, no." She wagged her head from side to side. "We're going to have the kids make their own tags."

"Okay…" I began tentatively, "so what's in the box?"

She began piling the contents upon my desk. "Here's some sandpaper, four wood burners, two portable vise clamps, a drill, safety goggles and 30 wood cookies."

"Right. So what's a wood cookie?"

I knew you'd ask about that, so I also threw in some samples for you to show your kids. My class finished their name tags yesterday."

I examined what appeared to be a thin slice of tree branch. "Do I get some in-service training for this project?" I asked her. "I've never used a drill before."

"Never?"

"Never."

"You mean to tell me you're 41 years old and

you've *never* used a drill?"

"I believe I've already answered that question."

Jo stared at me for a full 30 seconds before leaping into action. "I hope you're a quick study," she said. "School starts in 15 minutes." Deftly she donned the protective eyewear, clamped a board to the top of a desk and plugged in the drill.

While I watched her demonstration I thought about the little gaps and not-so-little chasms in my formal education. I grew up at a time when boys took wood shop and girls took Home Ec, when boys took auto shop and girls took Home Ec, when boys took drafting and girls took Home Ec.

(*Some might naturally assume, after all those Home Ec classes, that I'd be able to sew a button on straight, bake cinnamon rolls from scratch, and plan the menu for a decent seven course meal. Just remember, it never pays to assume too much…*)

There were no competent female role models wielding hammers or saws during my formative years. Other than Josephine the plumber, who occasionally graced the commercial airwaves, I cannot remember one single woman who knew how to use a wrench. The fact that I didn't know a Phillips from a flat head screwdriver until I was well into my twenties can undoubtedly be blamed on Harriet Nelson, June Cleaver and Donna Reed.

Determined not to let another day go by without my sixth grade boys *and* girls obtaining some practical hands-on experience, I carefully studied the tools Jo placed before me.

That school day came to a close with two dozen sanded, wood burned and drilled wooden name tags lined up neatly on my desk. All my children went home with a sense of accomplishment and pride. Even better, every child's fingers and thumbs were still intact.

Then last week, during the two and a half day sixth grade B.L.A.S.T. (*Building Leadership And Student Teamwork*) retreat, Jo asked me to assist her in the crafts room. "I need 17 holes drilled into each of 120 wooden disks for the bottoms of the cane baskets we'll be weaving," she said. "Think you can handle it?"

By the end of day two, there was sawdust everywhere. The majority of it appeared to be in my hair, ears and nose.

Jo smiled approvingly. "Tim Allen better watch out," she laughed. "Next thing you know, you'll be auditioning for a guest spot on Home Improvement's 'Tool Time.'"

"We'll have to see about that," I replied. "For now I'll be content to set a good example for my students. I have to admit though, I get kind of a rush brandishing this drill about. The hardest part is to keep from letting the 'power' in 'power tools' go straight to my head."

"Best to keep that in check," counseled Jo. "I don't think you'd want the kids referring to you as 'Madam Drillmeister.'"

"Maybe just in math class," I said, unable to resist the pun.

Jo ignored me and became thoughtful. "Let me ask you—hypothetically speaking, of course—if you were to get a tool belt or maybe your own set of tools for Christmas, what color would you choose for the handles?"

"Hypothetically speaking?" I grinned. "Any color but pink."

Under Construction

"I don't think we need to be speeding people through town," said a certain Long Beach City Councilor in January about the transportation plan for downtown. "We want them slowed down so they can see the town."

I hope she's happy.

Giving her the benefit of the doubt, she probably didn't have any idea how many road crews would be descending upon the Peninsula this spring when she uttered those fateful words.

Most of the rest of us are already tired of idling our engines while the sidewalks are being installed in Long Beach, the waterlines are hooked up in Chinook, the lights are going on in the tunnel, the bridge is re-painted, Sandridge gets paved, Highway 103 is widened, utilities are moved, potholes are filled, and a host of other traffic impediments provide us with wait time.

While sitting first in line (I'm sure I have the record for being first in line) at one of these construction sites, I pondered what it would be like to work on a road crew.

Yellow, slow. S-L-O-W. Red, stop. S-T-O-P. Point to the correct lane for vehicles to drive in. Bend the knees and press the air down with an open palm to slow traffic. Grin and wave. Try not to take it personally if drivers give you an international hand signal, unless it's the thumbs-up sign. Motion the traffic to follow the lead car. Talk on the headset. Whistle while you work.

I wonder what is taught in a flagger class. Do you get extra credit for working to raise flag brandishing to a new art form? Is there a prize for the most original choreography? Is there an award for Mr. or Ms. Congeniality? Are you taught how to keep from locking your knees and passing out?

While I could never spend even one hour on my feet flourishing a traffic control sign, I sometimes daydream about having a job that is over for the day when the whistle blows. A job that wouldn't follow me home.

"I know how you can find out what it's like," said one co-worker. "Have you noticed the good-looking flagger working with bridge crew?"

Noticed him? *Noticed him?* Just because I'm driving doesn't mean I'm blind to the scenic attractions along the route.

"Well," my colleague continued, "You could ask him. I hear he's the boss's son."

"Oh, yeah?" I stupidly replied, "How do you think he likes working for his dad?"

"Sexist!" my friend gloated, obviously enjoying my stumble into his trap. "Rumor has it that his mother runs the company."

Red-faced, I retreated, but not without taking note of the story possibilities contained in this exchange. If the information is correct, there's a feature article lurking in there somewhere. A woman road construction entrepreneur has the potential for a great non-traditional role model story.

Another daydream unfolds. . .

Suddenly, I swerve out of the line of traffic crossing the bridge, abandon my car and approach the flagger. It's a warm day, and his shirt is unbuttoned, exposing a muscular chest tanned by many months of outdoor labor. today he's not wearing gloves, and I can see that the third finger of his left hand is bare. I hand him a cold soda. . . our eyes meet. . . he tips his hard hat in appreciation, smiles, and. . . and. . . and I get out my trusty notebook to do an interview.

Gutless, I re-enter reality.

For starters, no one knows what really happens to people who pull out of line while following a lead car, because, as far as we know, no one has ever lived to tell about it. Secondly, what if I've been given false information?

I guess I'll have to play it safe and assign a couple of my writing students to do this particular interview. It'll give them practice, I'll find out what I need to know, and the *Observer* will get a fine feature article out of it. Everybody wins. Everybody, that is, except the poor motorist.

One of these nights we're going to turn on Letterman, or maybe Leno, and hear him say, "Do you know how far the line would reach if all the flaggers in Washington's Pacific County were laid end to end?"

And then they'll have to cut to commercial, cause nobody knows the answer to that question, not even a certain Long Beach City Councilor who finally got her way.

Baseball has been Very, Very Good to Me

Big Jeff stood at the plate, the bat resting casually on his right shoulder. Two strikes, two out, bottom of the third; he wasn't worried. Big Jeff was unarguably the best hitter we had. He was also our ace pitcher.

The opposing pitcher, shorter than Jeff by a least a foot, valiantly hurled the ball. It crossed the plate somewhere in the vicinity of Big Jeff's knees. "Strike three!" wailed the umpire.

Big Jeff sputtered in disbelief, his face turning neon pink. Kicking at the dirt in front of the grandstand, he muttered a decisively bad word.

Uncle Harry bolted from the dugout. There were two unalterable rules on his Little League team: no throwing bats, and no swearing. Any boy caught doing either one of these would be benched for the remainder of the game—no exceptions.

I sat in the first row of the grandstand, the official score book perched on my lap. With both hands, Uncle Harry grasped the chain-link fence separating us and stared me straight in the eye. "Did you hear what Jeff said?"

As a college sophomore home for a weekend of relaxation, I had unwittingly stumbled into the middle of a potentially nasty brouhaha. I met Uncle Harry's gaze and nodded. Behind me on the bleachers sat several dozen Little League parents.

Uncle Harry rephrased his question. "What, exactly, did Jeff say?" His eyes did not waver from mine. The crowd became silent. This could get ugly.

Reaching way down into my nineteen year old gift for equivocation, I called up information I learned in Speech 201. Little had I known at the time I had taken the class how important this knowledge would be. I took a deep breath.

In a voice loud enough for all to hear I said, "If I'm not mistaken, what Jeff said was an interdental, bilabial, unvoiced formative."

Uncle Harry took his hands from the fence. His eyes scanned the crowd, then he lifted his shoulders in an exaggerated shrug. "All that tuition money," he said, "finally paid off."

Big Jeff resumed the mound and we eventually won the game.

I thought a lot about Big Jeff while I watched the Mariners lose game six of the American League playoffs. Their own "Big Unit," Randy Johnson, undoubtedly had a few choice words of his own to say after that game. So did most everyone in Washington state.

Baseball, the great American pastime, finally came into its own in the Pacific Northwest. From out of the old growth timber slithered a flurry of fair weather fans, hungry for a team to boast about.

For many years I have claimed Seattle as "the land of my birth and the home of the Seahawks." I amended this statement to include the Mariners just a couple weeks ago, but I've been a baseball fan since I was old enough to swing a bat. I just didn't brag about it.

As a child, Uncle Harry took me to baseball games out in Sick's Stadium. I remember the Rainiers, the Angels and the Pilots. I remember the peanuts, the popcorn and the Cracker Jacks. And now, during a few short weeks this fall, the Mariners also became a team to remember, catapulting our corner of the world straight into the national spotlight.

Wherever I ventured between games last week, the talk centered on starting pitchers, batting line-ups and whether a fielder could redeem himself after an error shown over and over and over and over and over and over on countless sports programs.

Venturing out during the games was like being caught in a remake of *The Day the Earth Stood Still.*

"You'll just have to wait," said Nick at DC Video Connection. "The cash register only works between innings and during the commercials." Nick's my kind of fan.

Fifty-seven thousand other fans crowded the Kingdome for the last half-dozen games. Millions more became instant experts on RBIs, ERAs, and the disputed regulation height of the pitcher's mound. Governor Lowry went on record as vowing to keep Washington "a big-league state." (*I wonder how many games he snuck away to watch last spring...*)

No matter. Once a fan, always a fan, unless, of course, your team embarks on a particularly long losing streak. It's much easier to be a fan when you're winning.

And speaking of winning, how 'bout those Seahawks, huh? Ah, well, as in the race for the pennant, there's always next year.

Fuller Brush Girl

I trudged up the six rickety porch steps, plunked down my oversized brown vinyl briefcase and rapped tentatively on the screen door. I tried not to chew on my lower lip while I waited. Even after three months of door-to-door selling, my knees still quivered, my palms still got sweaty, and my heart still beat a rapid rhythm as I approached each house.

I heard water running in the kitchen followed by the clip-clop of hard-heeled shoes crossing the linoleum floor before the occupant appeared inside the screen. "Yes?" said an elderly woman in a floral print dress. She dried her hands on a gingham apron. "May I help you?"

Clearing my throat for the bazillionth time that day, I forced a lightness into my voice as I began my polished spiel: "Hi! I'm your Fuller Brush Girl, here with a free gift and a smile for you today!"

I held up my clenched right hand for the woman's perusal, just as I'd been taught at the sales meetings. A "free gift" was displayed between each knuckle: A plastic rain bonnet, folded neatly into its own small carrying case, a wire-handled pastry brush, a sturdy vegetable scrubber brush, and a plain black comb with the word "Fuller" stamped on the edge.

As the woman pushed the screen door aside a few inches to make her selection, I gave her my best ear-to-ear smile and held out a glossy brochure with my free hand. "If you have a minute, perhaps you'd like to browse through our sale catalog."

She sighed and shook her head. "I'm afraid I won't be buying anything from you. I have to live on a fixed income."

I acknowledged her statement with an understanding nod. "Thank you for your time," I said, turning to leave. "Have a nice day."

"Wait—" She reached out and gently touched my arm. "It's a hot day. You look like you could use some fresh-squeezed lemonade."

Gratefully, I accepted her offer. We sat and chatted like old friends on shady end of her front porch for the better part of two hours. I knew the crew boss wouldn't approve of me taking such a long break, but I also knew that he didn't have to know—I had garnered more than enough orders for one day.

As I stood to leave, the woman, still seated, fished around in her apron pocket and came up with a single dollar bill, folded into a small tight wad. Her words came out in a rush; she avoided my eyes. "You know I can't afford to buy anything, but I want you to have this dollar." She smoothed it out on her leg. "You've made an old lady happy just by sitting and visiting with me this afternoon. A lot of young people wouldn't have taken the time."

"I can't accept that."

"Of course you can, and you'd be doing me a favor, to boot." Her soft gray eyes now looked deep into my brown ones. Her head bobbed rapidly, adding emphasis to the words she spoke. "You told me a little bit ago that you were selling Fuller Brush to earn money for college."

"That's true."

"Well honey," she continued, "consider this a contribution to the cause. I always wanted to be able to send my own children to college, but I never could afford it. Only one of them ever amounted to much. But now you take this dollar from me and I'll be able to say I helped educate a future teacher. Here—" She took the empty lemonade glass from me and pressed the bill into my hand. "You put it in with your first quarter's tuition, and you become the best teacher you can learn how to be. We need good teachers."

There were so many things I could have said. Could have, but didn't. It's hard to speak when there's a lump in your throat the size of Nebraska…

All that was 25 years ago. Twenty-five years ago this week. And every year, as the college-bound students are leaving home to further their education, I've thought of that woman in the floral print dress and the gingham apron, and I've prayed that somehow she knew I never forgot the kindness she extended to a door-to-door Fuller Brush Girl on her way to becoming the best teacher she could learn how to be.

And I hope she'd have been proud.

The Barter System

"Just a minute, Tim," called Gene, striding across the parking lot. He slid open the side door of his van and pulled out a brown portfolio. Extracting a pen and ink and watercolor print, he autographed the bottom.
"Here, I want you to have this—consider it a tip—for that dynamite sax playing."

Tim shrugged. "I just happened to have my horn with me." He grinned. "I was surprised to find live blues being played in Ocean Park on a Sunday night. I just wanted to join in."

"Well, I want you to know how much I enjoyed it, " continued Gene. He handed Tim the print.

Not being the bashful type, I walked over uninvited and thumbed through Gene's artwork. "Hey," I said, "these are good! Would you consider trading me one of these prints for one of my books?"

"And I supposed you just happen to have your books with you?" interjected Tim.

I laughed. "We could set up our own bartering street fair. Where else but during a full moon at 2 a.m. in Grannie Annie's parking lot on a warm Sunday night in the middle of summer would you find a saxophone player who just happens to have his instrument with him, an artist who carries his work in his van, and a writer who totes her books around in her trunk?"

Where else indeed? But the more I thought about it,

the more I realized, except for the particular time of night when this particular transaction took place, the barter system is still very much a part of our economic foundation.

Bartering, the exchange of one commodity or service for another, appears frequently in our literary traditions. "I'll spin this straw into gold for you if you promise to give me your firstborn child," said Rumpelstiltskin to the damsel in distress, who eagerly accepted the proposed exchange rate without thought of negotiating a counter offer.

And then there was Jack, poor Jack, who traded a cow for a handful of magic beans. Now Jack may not have appeared to know beans about bartering, but his mother was no blue ribbon gardener, either. It's indeed fortunate those beans landed in fertile soil when she threw them out the window.

But it's a mixed blessing that I grew up in a household where bartering childhood chores was the norm. My complete lack of domesticity can undoubtedly be blamed on the fact that I traded all the inside jobs for the outside jobs. Instead of doing my fair share of the dishes, laundry and vacuuming, I earned my allowance car washing and lawn mowing. Mom didn't care who did it, as long as it got done.

"You were lucky," said my friend Anna Marie. "I'm an only child; there was no one to trade with." She set a slice of fresh-baked zucchini bread on the table before us. "You know," she continued, "if you would teach me how to use a computer, I could teach you how to cook."

"Who said I wanted to learn how to cook?"

"Okay," she countered, not ready to give up on the idea, "how about I teach you to grow a vegetable garden? My zucchini did *especially* well this year."

"What do I need vegetables for if I don't cook?"

"You're making this difficult," she said. "Why don't you just tell me— what do you want in trade for teaching me about the computer?"

"Your firstborn child."

"*You want Ricky?!*" asked Anna Marie incredulously.

"Actually," I hastened to explain, "I don't want Ricky so much as I want to borrow his toys."

"His toys?"

"It's a rather long story," I told her, "but the gist of it is that Liz likes to sew, and Carla had her make a set of drapes for their camper in exchange for six hours of babysitting."

"What's this got to do with Ricky's toys?"

"I told Carla I'd do the babysitting she owed Liz if I could get some help wallpapering the bathroom. But I don't have a lot of toys for kids that age to play with."

"I could teach you how to make six colors of play dough..." Anna Marie's smirk gave her away.

"I'm not falling for that."

"Hmm," she mused, buttering another slice of the warm bread. "How 'bout I take care of the babysitting and you give me the same number of hours of computer instruction *and* take two bags of zucchini off my hands?"

I think she's getting the hang of it.

CHAPTER 10
Multiple Personality Quirks

Crapstacking

Joe peeked tentatively into my home office and shook his head. "I suspected as much," he said. "Looks like you're a genuine crapstacker."

"I beg your pardon?"

"Crapstacking," he said, motioning to the piles upon piles of various assorted and sundry papers heaped on every available surface and sticking out of overflowing boxes filling the room. "A stack of crap here, a stack of crap there…yep, you're a crapstacker all right."

"I heard you the first time," I said, pulling the door shut. "I just didn't think you were the type of guy to criticize another person's system of organization."

"So I suppose you know just where everything is in there?" he asked.

"Well…" I hedged. "Almost."

"It's okay." Joe patted my arm. "You should see MY spare bedroom…"

Small consolation. Although misery allegedly loves company, it didn't make me feel any better to know I'm not the only crapstacker in the universe. I've been trying for years, yes *years*, to get my office unburied. I know there's a couch in there, and a table, and maybe a few chairs, but I haven't seen the carpet in so long that I can't remember what color it is.

"Start small," suggested my friend Anna Marie, surveying the room in question. "Just resolve to go through one pile each week."

"I tried that—I ended up restacking the stack I started with into four somewhat smaller mini-stacks and then stacking those stacks back together because I had nowhere to set them."

"What, exactly, is in all these piles that's so all-fired precious?"

"Just stuff I might need someday."

"For instance?"

"Look, you're getting awfully personal here… It's just stuff I'm not quite ready to throw out yet."

"Like mail order catalogs, birthday cards from three years ago and notes from an adult education class you taught in…" she paused to dig a little deeper into the collection nearest the door, "…in 1991?!"

"You never know…"

But I *do* know. Deep in my heart, I know I'll never, ever, not even in my wildest dreams, get my office clean enough for a "House Beautiful" photo shoot. I'm lucky to maintain a navigable path from the door to the computer.

"Do you suppose I could start a support group for crapstackers?" I asked Anna Marie while searching for the end of the plastic trash bag that opened. "Maybe something like 'Adult Children Suffering from Genetic Crapstacking Tendencies'?"

"You think crapstacking is *genetic*?"

"I gotta blame *somebody*… I don't think I developed this problem all by myself. When I was growing up, we had this hall closet…"

"It'll never fly," interrupted Anna Marie. "ACSGCT won't cut it. You need a catchy acronym. Something like MESSY KIDS."

"*That's* an acronym?"

"Mountains of Especially Stupid Stuff You Kept Instead of Discarding Sooner."

While I collapsed in a fit of laughter, Anna Marie continued, "*Everybody* has a hall closet, or a junk drawer, or a kitchen cupboard, or a couple boxes marked 'miscellaneous' stacked in the garage. The key is containment. You let the crap take over a whole room, and now it seems impossible to reclaim your territory."

"Have I ever told you about my great Aunt Flora? Now *there* was a crapstacker—"

"Jan," broke in Anna Marie, surveying what she could discern of my desk, "what's on all those disks?"

"Leave my disks alone."

"No, really, you must have 60 or 70 disks here." She scanned a dozen of them, her eyebrows arching upward. "And most of them aren't even labeled! Don't tell me you're into *electronic crapstacking* too?!"

I jerked the disks out of her hand. "Mind your own business."

"This is much worse than I thought," she said. "So tell me, has a 'chat line' been established yet for crapstackers? Are you into storing heretofore worthless pieces of information you've downloaded from other compulsive savers?"

"Thank you for your concern," I said, pointing her toward the door, "but I think I'd rather tackle this by myself."

"Isn't there some kind of a Macintosh prompt that asks if you want to 'Save' each time you work on the computer?"

"Of course."

"Then why don't you personalize your software by changing it to read "Is this crap really worth saving?' Honestly, Jan, don't you know why you have a 'delete' button? There's an endless supply of junk e-mail—you don't have to save all this crap!"

"*Good-bye*, Anna Marie."

"Wait!" she said, as I escorted her outside, "you could create a Home Page for people just like you—something like 'http://www.crapstak.com'."

I wonder what Joe would say about that.

Solitary Confinement

Last Saturday evening, at exactly 9:35 p.m. Pacific daylight savings time, in an unprecedented stroke of fortitude, I accomplished a feat of strength heretofore unimaginable: I deleted my computer solitaire program from my hard drive.

At 10:45 I reinstalled it.

By 1:15 a.m. I had played another 25 rounds of "Forty Thieves," bringing the total number of games played since Christmas to an even 1,832. According to the program data, I had won 186 times, or, I discovered after using the built-in calculator, approximately one game out of every 9.8494623656 tries.

This got me to thinking. One hand of this game takes roughly six minutes to play. That's about 10 games an hour. One thousand eight hundred thirty-two games translates into 183.2 hours of solitaire played in the past six months.

It didn't take much math to figure out that I had devoted an average of an hour a day to this mindless activity. In the beginning, I was using the game solely to "relax" before turning in for the evening. Better than taking a sleeping pill, I rationalized. But I knew there were many nights when I read myself to sleep instead. Which means, of course, that frequently when I turned on the machine I ended up playing the game for two or maybe even three hours straight.

"It's not like I'm obsessed or anything," I told my friend Anna Marie, the following afternoon. "It's just that I like to play it when I'm all wound up and don't want to try concentrating on anything more meaningful."

"Or when you're procrastinating," said the ever-wise Anna Marie. "Admit it, Jan, you're hooked on that silly game. You know you could spend your time working on something else but—"

"Enough! Can't a person play a harmless little game of solitaire without the world coming to an end?"

"You're the one who brought it up," she said. "So you must realize it's not all that harmless. It sounds like it's become a real problem for you. Think of all the other things you could have accomplished if you hadn't been glued to the computer screen for hours and hours clicking the mouse arrow on card after card."

I glared at her.

Anna Marie broke the silence. "Have you considered joining a support group?"

"A support group?! It's not like I'm addicted to the darn game!"

"Isn't it?" she asked. "Let's be honest about this. The first step is admitting that you are powerless over computer solitaire."

"First step?! The next thing I know, you'll want me to call up all the people I let leave messages on the answering machine last week and admit that I didn't take their calls because I was too involved in a hot card game!"

"Jan," said Anna Marie, taking my hand, "this is much more serious than I thought. I think it's time you bit the bullet and got rid of that program for good."

"Cold turkey?"

"Cold turkey." She looked me straight in the eye. "And don't even think about saving it on a disk. You don't need the temptation in the house."

She was right, of course. We went immediately into my home office, put the game into the Macintosh "trash" and cleared it from my hard drive. Reluctantly, I gave her the installation disk.

"You can thank me when your next book comes out," she said as she left a short time later. "Now you are free to spend your time at the computer doing some serious writing."

I walked back into the office and sat down in front of the keyboard for a few minutes. Then I went to the kitchen and made a sandwich. Next I reorganized my hard drive files by name, then icon, then date, and finally reverted to listing them by name again. I shuffled listlessly through several stacks of disks piled on my desk.

A green label caught my attention. The writing on it wasn't in my handwriting. It was marked "Finger Food."

I trembled as I inserted it into the disk drive where I discovered, much to my horror and delight, that it contained more than a dozen assorted computer games, ranging from "Shanghai" to "Concentration" and "MacYahtzee" to a casino slot machine game called, appropriately enough, "MacBandit."

Anna Marie called bright and early the next morning. "So how's it going?" she asked. "Any solitaire withdrawal symptoms?"

"I didn't miss it a bit." I yawned audibly into the phone. "Not one single bit."

To Thine Own Self Be True

"Forty-eight hours," said Bill. "I'll tell you in 48 hours."

"Tell me now," I begged. "I might die within 48 hours and then I'd never know."

"And you wouldn't need to know, either."

One of the things I like best about Bill is his sense of logic. At least I used to. I tease him about being hopelessly analytic but it's one of the reasons we've been friends so long. Bill enjoys dealing with facts; he disects even the smallest details. And while I react to situations on a more emotional level, I can always count on him to give me a clear perspective from the flip side of the coin.

Bill and I only get together every few months, yet I consider him among my best male friends. He never hesitates to make time, where there usually isn't any, for what's truly important. And what Bill finds truly important are his friends.

Throughout the years I've come to appreciate Bill's strengths and weaknesses, his humor, wit, and intelligence. We've conversed about harmonics, quarks, time and space warps, homeopathic healing, investment opportunities, and existentialism. But this time our talk hit a little closer to home.

"Why can't you just tell me now?" I asked again. "It's not like you to play games. Spit it out."

"Nope." He shook his head. "I want you to really

think about this. If you think about it hard enough, you might get it all by yourself."

"Look Bill, I didn't come here for analysis. As I recall, we were talking about self-actualization and personal autonomy."

"That's correct," conceded Bill. "And I simply said I didn't think a person can accomplish either goal until he or she can identify, and learn to captialize upon, his or her best and worst personality traits."

"Do you realize you're one of the few people I know who don't mangle their sentences using 'he or she' and 'his or her'?"

"Nice try at a segue."

"Thanks." I grinned sheepishly. "But you're not going to let me off the hook, are you?"

"Of course not. What kind of a friend would I be if I let you change the subject every time you were uncomfortable with the topic?"

"A compassionate friend."

He laughed, but continued the inquisition. "Come on, Jan, focus. What do you think I think is the most unattractive thing about you?"

There were so many choices. So very many choices. I took a deep breath. "Do you think it's the way I like to be 'in control' of most situations?"

"No," he said, "but that's a good one. Except I see your compulsion for control as an indication of strong leadership skills."

"That's it!" I fairly jumped out of the chair. "You think I'm obsessive/compulsive! That's what you see as my worst personality trait!"

"Wrong again. What you call 'obsessive/compulsive' I see only as an attempt at perfectionism. There's nothing wrong with trying to do everything right. You just have to accept that no matter how much you stew about it, some things aren't ever going to be perfect."

"Ah ha! You've just given me another clue... Could it be that I worry too much?"

"It could be, but that isn't what I had in mind."

My frustration reached the saturation point. "Well then, Mr. Know-It-All, could your name be Rumpelstiltskin?"

"Huh?"

I sighed a long, slow, exaggerated sigh. "I'm tired of this game, Bill, just tell me what you think."

"Call me in 48 hours." He walked me to the door. "You can call sooner if you think you've figured it out."

It was a long 48 hours. The first day I called six times to venture guesses. The second day I resolved not to give him the satisfaction of hearing me expound on my foibles.

Forty-five hours. Forty-six. Forty-seven. Forty-seven hours, 30 minutes. Forty-seven hours, 45 minutes. Forty-seven hours, 50 minutes. Forty-seven hours, 51 minutes. Fifty-two minutes, 53, 54, 55. Maybe if I dialed very, very slowly...

Bill answered on the first ring. "Remember," he began, "even when I tell you what I think is your worst personality trait, it won't do you any good unless you use that information to help you get closer to your goal of self-actualization and autonomy."

"Yes, yes, I'll remember!" I shouted into the phone. "Cut the chatter and get to the point! *Just tell me*!"

"In my opinion," said Bill, "the trait you really need to work on is being a little more patient."

Going, Going, Going…Gray!

"Blasphemy!" my incredulous friend Googie fairly shouted, slamming her latte down with a jolt. "You can't be serious," she continued, reaching for the napkins to mop the tabletop. "In all the time I've known you, I've never heard you say anything quite so ridiculous."

"I'm 41," I sighed. "Who do I think I'm kidding?"

"Why do you want to look older than you have to? Next thing I know, you'll probably be telling me you also want to start acting your age."

"How can I?" I countered. "Not only do I not know what 41 looks like, but I have no idea what 41 acts like."

"Trust me," said Googie, "you won't like either one."

"I am what I am," I replied, "my mind is made up. As of today, I'm not going to color my hair any more."

The decision was not made lightly; since 1989 I'd grown accustomed to this pre-fabricated hair color. That was the year my mother, sorting through boxes of great Aunt Flora's saved letters, came across a curl of my hair, tied with a bright red ribbon. The curl commemorated my first real haircut, snipped the day before I began kindergarten 30 years prior.

I took the clipping to my hairdresser. "Match this," I told her, "then if anyone asks if my hair is my natural color, I can look them squarely in the eye and answer affirmative." And so for the past seven years I've been

Clairol #35, Sunset Brown, the hair color of quite an adorable little five year old. Or so I've been told.

"As far as I can figure," I said, once again addressing Googie, "the only one my age who doesn't have gray hair is Barbie—and she's as plastic and synthetic as they come."

"You're grasping at straws," said Googie. "What's really behind this?"

"I just don't think American women should let themselves be brainwashed by the advertising media to believe that appearance is more important than intelligence, that gray hair makes one less desirable, or that maturity is something to be camouflaged. I'd like to see the hair color companies all go out of business because women everywhere are satisfied with who and what they are."

"Whoa, girlfriend," said Googie. "I hope you don't get a nosebleed way up there on that soapbox of yours." She took another swallow of coffee. "You make it sound like any woman who colors her hair should be convicted of fraud. Do you realize you're condemning some of your very best friends?"

Of course I hadn't thought of that. I wasn't even sure if I had convinced myself that this decision was really in my best interest. But a friend is someone with whom one can safely think aloud; I was merely testing out the strength of my resolve.

While still pondering, Googie's daughter Lavida returned from the store. My mouth dropped open as I observed her putting away groceries. "Your hair is orange." It was a statement that needed no response, and no response was exactly what I got. "Is this the flavor of the week?" I continued.

Before Lavida could reply, her mother cut in. "Jan's going through an au naturel phase. I suspect it'll pass. She must be interested in an older guy, or found a younger guy who likes older women, or something like that."

"Don't talk about me like I'm not here!" I said.

"Well, maybe I don't think you are all here." Googie smiled sympathetically. "I still don't understand your motivation for wanting to look older than necessary."

"I really thought you'd be the one person who'd support me on this." I shook my head. "Why should I waste time and money to try to look any younger than I am? My self-esteem is not tied all that tightly to what color my hair is. Maybe the resistance I'm encountering is due to the fact that my nearly same-age friends are afraid they'll be guilty by association."

"That's where you're wrong," said Googie. "Some of your friends will die before ever admitting to a single gray hair."

"That's easy for you to say; you're blonde. Any gray hair you get will never show.

"What makes you think I was blonde at birth?" she said softly.

"Blasphemy!" I fairly shouted, knocking my empty latte cup over as I bolted to the bathroom for a quick peek in the mirror. "Tell me the truth now, Googie," I hollered back out to her, "just how do you think I'd look as a blonde?"

The Emergency Xerox™ Box

"I thought you had company coming," said Anna Marie, pouring our third or fourth cup of tea.

"Are you trying to get rid of me?"

"Of course not. I just thought it was odd you'd have time to stop by for a visit today. You're usually in such a panic to clean the house before anyone's allowed to see it."

"The house," I informed her, "is spotless." I stared thoughtfully into my mug before continuing. "That's why I can't go home yet—I don't want to risk messing it up."

I guess I'm one of those quasi-perfectionist types. In my rational mind, I know that friends come to visit the PERSON, not the house. But in the other part of my brain, the part that was hopelessly warped at a very tender age, I can still hear my mother's admonition:

"Don't even *think* about going to bed in the evening without tidying up the house. If the Queen of England arrives before you're out of bed in the morning, you wouldn't want to be caught with clutter everywhere, would you?"

Mother never cottoned to my suggestion that if the Queen of England arrived without calling first she *deserved* to have to step over yesterday's discarded newspapers.

"So where'd you stash everything this time?" asked Anna Marie. "I know perfectly well you didn't actually put all that junk piled on the dining room table away where it rightfully belongs. Come on Jan, which closet did you cram the new Xerox box into?"

The Xerox box. Years ago, in a moment of weakness, I confessed the secret of the Xerox box to Anna Marie. Hedging was pointless; she knew me too well.

"I stuck it in the back bathroom shower."

Anna Marie raised her 'tell me more' eyebrow.

"The hall closets are both full," I continued, "and so is the crawlspace under the stairwell and the extra cupboard in the kitchen—Don't look at me like that!—I don't use the back shower anyway."

Although it's true my grandmother hailed directly from England, where, I was told, the Queen herself could be expected to drop in for tea at any time, the inherited gene for pristine orderliness did not continue beyond my mother. To compensate, I hired the most wonderful cleaning lady to bail me out of the chaos twice a month.

I lose a lot a sleep the night before my cleaning lady comes. Maneuvering the bulldozer and fire hose through the house to clear a trail through the major debris takes a lot of time. But for the miscellaneous 'little stuff' the Xerox box never fails me; it's quick and effective.

Where I work there is an endless supply of sturdy cardboard boxes initially used to transport 10 reams of paper for the copier. We refer to these boxes as 'Xerox boxes,' although neither the copier nor the paper bears the registered trademark.

I have found, through trial and error, that by placing a Xerox box at one end of the dining room table and lifting the other end of the tablecloth high over my head, all the clutter slides right into the box. Then I store it safely away to be sorted through some other time.

Unfortunately, Anna Marie once observed this process. She said nothing at the time, but I still feel the guilt of my English ancestry. "I only use Xerox boxes in real emergencies," I lied. "The morning my cleaning lady is due it's essential to get as much as possible out of her way."

"You mean you clean *before* she cleans? ...That's crazy."

"She wouldn't know what to do with all the piles of papers and stacks of stuff. It would be like asking her to read my mind to leave it spread across the tables and counters."

"You could tell her to ignore it."

"But then I'd come home and the house wouldn't look *clean.* What would be the point?"

"Well," said Anna Marie, "do you at least *label* the boxes?"

"Label them?" I asked incredulously. "You mean with a felt pen or something? I... I don't remember which box my markers are in."

Anna Marie shook her head. "So when do you expect your company to arrive?"

"Any time now. In case they show up before I do, I left them a note to make themselves at home."

"What makes you think they won't mess up the house before you get there?" smirked Anna Marie.

"They won't," I laughed, "they're from England."

A Burning Desire

"Have I ever introduced you to my father?" asked Ken.

"Your father?" I repeated.

"My father," he said again. "He resides here."

I glanced quickly around the room. Ken and I had known each other for several years. This was the first time he'd mentioned his father sharing living quarters with him.

"I'm sorry." I shook my head. "For some reason I thought you told me your father had passed away."

"He has." Ken pointed to a cardboard container (a.k.a. *urn*) on the top shelf of the bookcase. "Jan," he said, "I'd like you to meet my dad..."

Mortality is not something I like to spend a lot of time dwelling upon. Especially my own. But right around the anniversary of my birth, I often get to thinking about the passing of time, which naturally leads me to thinking about the passing of people. This year was no exception.

First I took a hard look at my last will and testament and made a few minor adjustments. Then I invited my good friend Anna Marie over for tea.

"I want you to promise me something," I began.

"Sure. What do you need?"

"Promise me you won't let anybody play a long, drawn-out, bazillion-verse rendition of 'Amazing Grace' at my funeral."

Anna Marie remained silent. I took that as consent

and continued, "And promise me that you'll see to it I'm cremated."

She spoke slowly and carefully, pausing briefly between each word, "You...want...to...be...cremated?"

"Yeah. I couldn't decide which outfit to be buried in, and I wasn't sure who'd get to make that decision. Cremation seemed like a logical alternative."

"You're serious about this."

"Deathly serious—uh, no pun intended. I figured it would save everybody a lot of trouble if I made as many of these decisions as possible ahead of time. Hopefully, wayahead of time."

"You mean to tell me you don't want me to do your make-up for you?"

"No way. You'd probably want to do something dumb, like put glitter on my eyelids."

"What's the matter with adding a touch of sparkle?" asked Anna Marie, exaggeratedly batting her purple lashes in my direction. "And what brought all this up, anyway? Are you ill?"

"Actually, I feel great. But none of us knows for sure what will happen tomorrow. I called the mortuary, and—"

"*You called the mortuary*?!"

"Sure did. Talked to someone named Ron. Real nice guy."

Anna Marie raised her eyebrows way up near her hairline. "Jan, you never cease to amaze me."

"Look, if you want to know something, you ask an expert. *Anyway*," I continued, "I need you to swear to me that you'll claim my ashes in a timely manner and scatter them appropriately."

"And where, pray tell, do you want them scattered?"

"This has been causing me some concern. The ocean, although handy, is highly over-rated. Salt spray, soggy carnations and endless rolling waves is not all that romantic. Besides, I get seasick. So next I thought about the mountains, but I ruled that out too. One of the reasons I moved to the peninsula was because I dislike the cold—particularly snow."

Anna Marie closed her eyes and shook her head.

"And I definitely do not wish to be sprinkled in anybody's flower bed or back yard. That's what they did to my uncle. Now every time Aunt Susan mows her lawn, she's got Uncle Tony flying up in her face." I paused to take a sip of tea. "And please, *please* don't think you need to keep me on a shelf in your living room."

"No problem," said Anna Marie. "So… exactly what DO you want done with your remains?"

"I'm still working on that. In the meantime, I've decided to produce my own eulogy video."

Anna Marie spit tea clear across the kitchen. "You're kidding, right?"

"Wrong. I figure I'm entitled to say a few well-chosen words, recite some of my own poetry, even sing if I want to, and nobody would dare be so disrespectful as to walk out on my final performance."

"A self-styled karaoke eulogy? That's macabre."

"I've made up my mind, and there's only one thing that'll keep me from following through with it."

"A power outtage?"

"No." I glowered at her. "I know it's a long shot, but maybe, just maybe, I'll live forever."

"It's a long shot all right," said Anna Marie, rising to her feet. "Fix me another cup of tea, and I'll go get the camcorder."

The Sound of Music

"Why haven't I heard you play the piano?" asked the ever-inquisitive Anna Marie.

"Because I don't play the piano."

"Then why is there a piano in your rec room?"

"I needed something to hold up the candelabra."

I bought that piano with my first paycheck after moving to the beach. For twenty years it's been a not-so-subtle reminder of my limitations. No matter how much I think I want to learn to play, I can never quite get beyond six months of frustration before I toss in the towel.

At fifteen, high school sports took precedence over practice. My college sweetheart, a superb saxophone player, tried to teach me the basics, but the relationship was fraught with flats and sharps.

Where there's a will, there's a way, I told myself, and in my early thirties I attempted a third time to make sense out of reading music. Although the adage "You can't teach an old dog new tricks" beat a steady rhythm in my brain, I found an instructor who could accommodate my work schedule and plunged ahead with lessons.

But try as I may, my left hand never seemed to know what my right hand was up to. Or vice versa. I tried to make light of it by saying, "I just washed my hands, and I can't do a thing with them." It didn't help that my instruction book was called "Teaching Little Fingers to Play."

Had I begun learning music in elementary school, I might have had a chance. But there were four of us kids, extremely close in age, and band instruments just weren't in the budget.

Music, however, was always a part of our lives. We often sang during long car trips, most likely more to keep us from squabbling than preserving our heritage, yet both objectives were accomplished.

"You Are My Sunshine," "Oh Suzanna," "Down by the Old Mill Stream" "Polly Wolly Doodle," "De Camptown Races," and "I Been Working on the Railroad" intermingled with songs from World War II and FDR's New Deal.

For years I thought Seattle had only one radio station. Mother set all five buttons to "K-A-Y-O, one-one-five-oh, country western on your radio dial." When she was in the car, it was country western or nothing.

That all changed one special Sunday night when I was nine years old. Mom stood in the darkened doorway. "Jan," she whispered, softer than soft, "are you still awake?"

My younger sister and I shared a bedroom. Sometimes, after I was sure she was asleep, I was allowed to slip out of bed and get back up for an hour or so. Being the oldest had its advantages.

This particular Sunday night I crept from under the covers, just minutes from being asleep myself, and tip-toed down the hall. The Ed Sullivan Show was on TV.

"I wanted you to see this," said Mom, motioning for me to join her on the couch. "It's that group from England—the Beatles."

"She loves you, ya, ya, ya… She loves you, ya, ya, ya…" What kind of crazy lyrics were those? Certainly not any that Jim Reeves, Johnny Cash or Lefty Frizzell might be caught singing. And their *hair*!

I took a good look at my mother. My *mother* seemed to be enjoying this assault on our ears. She sat smiling and tapping her foot. Back on the screen the camera panned the audience— screaming, crying, frantic teen-aged women tearing at their own hair and jumping up and down like a bunch of lunatics. If they weren't careful, I thought, they'd completely drown out the performers.

At the end of the show, I headed back to bed without being told. "So what did you think?" asked Mom.

I shrugged. How could I tell her I didn't understand all the fuss over these four long-hairs from Liverpool? And how could I tell my mom I thought she was too old to go for this kind of music? After all, if I was nine, and she was 22 when I was born, then she must have been… she must have been… 31.

And now I'm 42.

My music taste broadened considerably in years between junior high school and 35. And then I hit the wall. I never liked rap, all of Hootie's songs sound the same, and when I want to smash pumpkins I'm content to wait for Halloween.

The piano, however, still holds some appeal. Maybe it's not too late.

Just Follow the Bouncing Ball

It was one of those nights. Not 'dark and stormy,' just dark. Winter dark. And the moon, well, I have a tendency to blame a lot of my mischief on the phases of the moon…

"Let's hop the creek," said Anna Marie.

"Huh?" (Note that this was not one of my snappier come-backs.)

"Let's go south of the border."

"Mexico?"

"Astoria."

"Yeah, sure." I readily agreed. "I need a few things from Costco and Freddy's."

"I'm not talking about *shopping*," sighed Anna Marie, "I'm talking about a night out in another town—let's go check out some new places, new faces."

So we checked out a couple places in Hammond. And Warrenton. And one or two in Astoria. It was still fairly early.

"How 'bout the House of Chan?" asked Anna Marie.

"Hold it." I stopped with my hand on the door. "It's karaoke night. I tried it once—and discovered I really don't enjoy making a fool of myself."

"Aw, come on, be a good sport."

Good sportsmanship goes only so far. Seating myself at the bar, I flipped disinterestedly through the karaoke song book before setting it aside. "I'm the designated driver," I told the bartender. "I won't be singing tonight."

Anna Marie sat next to a man who immediately began telling her all about his voice lessons and the best microphone techniques. A few minutes later, a fellow wearing shorts sat on the stool next to mine. He ordered a drink and handed the bartender a neatly written list of Chinese food items.

"My name's Tom," he said, turning to address me. "I have a great wife and two terrific daughters and I just came in to pick up a take-out order."

"Why are you telling me all this?" I asked, shaking the hand he offered.

"Well, I didn't want you to think—"

"Whoa, boy!" I interrupted him. "We're in a *bar. I know better* than to think."

He laughed.

"Here," I said, pushing the song book in front of him, "you can sing for your supper."

"I love to sing," said Tom. "But I'm not very good at it. You should hear my wife—she sings really, really well."

"Your wife's not here," I said. "It's up to you."

"I'll sing if you sing," he countered.

"Sure thing," I replied. "You go first."

The karaoke host, I'll call her Prancy, was, until then, singing the majority of songs herself. She was decked out in '40's garb, complete with layers of taffeta and a little shell of a hat pinned to her hair.

"It's time to give her a break," said Mr. Voice Lessons. He handed her a slip of paper with some cue numbers written on it.

Here it comes, I thought. *I'm going to have to sit here and smile and pretend to appreciate his singing. I wonder if it would be too obvious if I bolted for the restroom.*

An Elvis song appeared on the screen. Mr. Voice Lessons opened his mouth. I cringed in anticipation. But before the night was over, Anna Marie and I begged him to sing every Elvis song in the book.

Sometimes the magic works. Sometimes the frogs really are princes. And sometimes, when the night is winter dark and the moon is, well, the moon is right there in the sky, I begin to remember what it's like to believe in magic.

I found three or four songs in the guide that I thought I knew all the words to. I filled out the request paper. Then I went to the bathroom.

All too soon, Prancy placed the microphone in my sweaty hands. Mr. Voice Lessons signaled for me to hold it closer to my mouth. And when the song finally ended, 20 or 30 hours later, people I didn't even know clapped for me.

"Are they applauding because I've stopped singing?" I asked Anna Marie.

"No," said Mr. V.L. "You did fine."

And then one man bought me a soda. And another man put his arm around me and kissed my cheek. And that's all it took.

I sang to my little heart's content. Never mind that my knees shook the entire time, I was having FUN—the kind of fun that is unexpected, spontaneous and truly joyful.

It didn't matter if we all san, or if we laughed so hard that *nobody* sang. The only thing that mattered was that a few people, for a few hours, managed to pack up their troubles in their old kit bags and sing, sing, sing.

"Look at that moon," said Anna Marie as we crossed the bridge heading home, "I love the way it reflects on the water."

"Moon River." I smiled. "I think we could sing that..."

ABOUT THE AUTHOR

Long Beach, Washington, author Jan Bono wrote a humorous, personal experience newspaper column from 1992 to 2002. These columns garnered 11 state awards from the Washington State Newspaper Association. The first volume of Through My Looking Glass" was published in 1995 by Kaleidoscope Press. It was high time for Volume II! Jan has written for various national publications, from Guidepost to Woman's World. She has seen over a dozen of her one-act plays performed and has published several short story collections. Watch for her first novel, a mystery set on the Southwest Washington Coast!

See more of Jan's work at: www.JanBonoBooks.com